creating
# Keepsakes

# EASIER-THAN-EVER
## Scrapbooking Treasury

You and Sarah haven't haven't been friends for very long, but you sure did click right from the start. You both have such similar fun and energetic personalities that it was impossible for you not to become fast friends. You have quite the crush on Ms. Sarah and the feeling is definitely mutual.

new FRIENDS

A LEISURE ARTS PUBLICATION

## Creating Keepsakes

**Editor-in-Chief:** Jennafer Martin

**Founding Editor:** Lisa Bearnson

**Managing Editor:** Lara Penrod

**Creative Editor:** Megan Hoeppner

**Senior Editor:** Kim Jackson

**Editor:** Lori Fairbanks

**Associate Editors:**
Dorathy Gilchrist, Joannie McBride

**Online Senior Editor:** Amber Ellis

**Online Editor:** Erin Weed

**Editorial Assistant:** Ahtanya Johnson

**Art Director:** Erin Bayless

**Senior Designer:** Neko Carillo

**Contributing Designer:** Gaige Redd

**Photography:**
BPD Studios, Vertis Communications

Library of Congress Control Number:
2011935915
ISBN-13/EAN: 978-1-60900-382-1

## Creative Crafts Group, LLC.

**President and CEO**
Stephen J. Kent

**VP/Group Publisher**
Tina Battock

**President of Book Publishing**
W. Budge Wallis

**Chief Financial Officer**
Mark F. Arnett

**Corporate Controller**
Jordan Bohrer

**VP/Publishing Director**
Joel P. Toner

**VP/Production**
Barbara Schmitz

**VP/Circulation**
Nicole McGuire

**VP/e-Media**
Eric Svenson

**Associate Publisher**
Barb Tanner

**Production Manager**
Michael Rueckwald

## Leisure Arts

**Vice President and Editor-in-Chief**
Susan White Sullivan

**Director of Designer Relations**
Cheryl Johnson

**Special Projects Director**
Susan Frantz Wiles

**Senior Prepress Director**
Mark Hawkins

**Imaging Technician**
Stephanie Johnson

**Prepress Technician**
Janie Marie Wright

**Publishing Systems Administrator**
Becky Riddle

**Mac Information
Technology Specialist**
Robert Young

**President
and Chief Executive Officer**
Rick Barton

**Vice President of Sales**
Mike Behar

**Director of Finance & Administration**
Laticia Mull Dittrich

**National Sales Director**
Martha Adams

**Creative Services**
Chaska Lucas

**Information Technology Director**
Hermine Linz

**Controller**
Francis Caple

**Vice President, Operations**
Jim Dittrich

**Retail Customer Service Manager**
Stan Raynor

**Print Production Manager**
Fred F. Pruss

Published by Leisure Arts, Inc., 5701 Ranch Drive, Little Rock, Arkansas 72223-9633. 501-868-8800. www.leisurearts.com.

# Easier-than-Ever
## Scrapbooking Treasury

## contents

# "recipes" save you time

Between spending time with family and friends, and making time for work and play, we're all incredibly busy these days. What would you do if you suddenly found yourself with some extra time? I don't know about you, but I can think of lots of ways I'd love to spend an extra hour or two. And whether you'd spend that time by yourself or with loved ones, I'm sure you'd value such a precious gift. Well, that's just what following the time-saving "scrapbooking recipes" in this book will give you!

While the 183 no-fail recipes for easy and beautiful scrapbook layouts in this book can't help with all of the demands on your time, it can definitely simplify scrapbooking, which will give you a bit more time in your busy schedule. With a few staple supplies you most likely already have on hand and your own creative flair, you can "cook up" amazing pages in whatever time you have. Just check the handy time guidelines— each layout takes anywhere from 20 minutes to about an hour—to create an eye-catching layout in a time frame that fits your schedule.

By taking the guesswork out of layout design, these layout recipes will give you valuable leftovers: time! And the best part? You can spend that time making or scrapbooking more memories! We hope you enjoy the scrapbook ideas in this book and find it a valuable resource in your busy life.

Enjoy!

Jennafer Martin
Editor-in-Chief
*Creating Keepsakes* magazine

P.S. Look for this icon `4×6` throughout the book for layouts created entirely with uncropped 4" x 6" photos!

TOTAL TIME TO SCRAPLIFT:

## 45 minutes

## from the pantry

- ☐ 3 sheets cardstock
- ☐ 2 sheets patterned paper (glitter and shaped)
- ☐ 1 set epoxy letter stickers (including numerals)
- ☐ 1 epoxy sticker accent
- ☐ ½ yard ribbon
- ☐ 1 pen
- ☐ 6 photographs

## just add

- ☐ 3 decorative pins
- ☐ 2 rhinestones

Pumpkins by Megan Hoeppner. **Supplies** *Cardstock:* Stampin' Up! (green) and Wausau Paper (purple); *Patterned paper:* Doodlebug Design (orange glitter) and Making Memories (lined); *Ribbon and epoxy stickers:* American Crafts; *Rhinestones:* Doodlebug Design; *Decorative pins:* K&Company; *Other:* Pen.

## INSTRUCTIONS

1 Trim and affix patterned paper to left side of layout. Mat a block of five photos with green and orange papers and attach to right hand page. Add photo atop lined paper.

2 Apply ribbon between photo lines. Add small section of patterned paper to bottom right of layout.

3 Adhere title letters, rhinestones, pins and epoxy accents. Handwrite journaling.

## make it (even) easier!

Mat your photos just once to save a step.

# let's get cookin'!

I love to bake and cook. But I have a few stipulations before I get out my pots and pans:

1. I have to use a recipe.

2. The item I'm making can only use a few ingredients (five or less is my favorite).

3. The recipe has to use staples I already have on hand. (I'm not into running around town trying to find one ingredient.)

4. It has to be quick with a lot of flavor.

My scrapbooking style is similar. I follow a few guidelines each time I make a page:

1. I use a recipe. I either find a page by another scrapbooker that I can use as a blueprint, or I sketch my own.

2. My favorite pages use only a few ingredients.

3. Rarely do I go to a scrapbook store looking for the perfect embellishments—I use what I have on hand.

4. My pages usually take less than an hour to create.

If you have similar guidelines when you set out to scrapbook, you've come to the right place. This book takes us all back to what's really important—photos and journaling, and saving time and money. On page 8, we give you a list of "pantry" supplies to use, then give you idea after idea on how to use them.

For example, on the layout to the right, I used 4" x 6" pictures that were developed at the photo lab. I quickly trimmed several of the photos and placed some to form a collage on my white mat and arranged a few more in a vertical line by my patterned paper. Having my photos already printed was a huge time- and money-saver. I also used basics from my stash—stickers, chipboard shapes, patterned paper and cardstock.

Have fun as you rediscover supplies you already have on hand. This will give you more time to spend with your family and to bake that luscious double-chocolate cake. Make sure you share the recipe with me!

*Lisa Bearnson*

TOTAL TIME TO SCRAPLIFT:

## 45 minutes

## from the pantry

☐ 5 sheets cardstock

☐ 1 sheet patterned paper (circles)

☐ 4 chipboard shapes

☐ 1 set dimensional letter stickers

☐ 7 stickers

☐ 1 pen

☐ 12 photographs

**Lake Powell** by Lisa Bearnson. **Supplies** *Cardstock:* Bazzill Basics Paper; *Patterned paper:* American Crafts; *Chipboard shapes and stickers:* June 2008 Kit, *KitoftheMonth.com; Pen:* Slick Writer, American Crafts.

## INSTRUCTIONS

1 Crop photos to create collage and mat on white paper. Adhere to right side of layout. Affix strip of patterned paper to left edge of layout. Crop and add line of photos to right of strip.

2 Attach six fish accents to white paper, mat with blue and apply to left page. Add three fish accents to right page and layer chipboard embellishments at top left of layout.

3 Create title with letter stickers, and handwrite journaling.

## make it (even) easier!

Instead of matting the fish accents, simply place a plain piece of contrasting cardstock behind them.

# the scrapbooking pantry: what's on hand

Before we get "cooking," let's check out what we've got in our cupboard. These stock items are the basic supplies needed to create the layouts and cards in this book. Your pantry may differ slightly, so feel free to make substitutions as you desire. It's all delicious!

**SHELF 1:**

1 Brads

2 Chipboard accents

3 Stamps (letters/numbers and shapes)

4 Stamping ink

5 Paint

**SHELF 2:**

6 Embroidery floss or thread

7 Ribbon/trims

8 Letter stickers (flat and dimensional)

9 Decorative stickers (flat and dimensional)

10 Pens

11 Rub-ons (letters/ numbers and decorative)

**SHELF 3:**

12 Cardstock

13 Patterned paper (variety—including laser-cut, textured and scallop-edged)

14 Computer for journaling and titles

7GYPSIES, AMERICAN CRAFTS, BASICGREY, BAZZILL BASICS PAPER, BO-BUNNY PRESS, CLOSE TO MY HEART, COLORBÖK, DAISY D'S PAPER CO., DIE CUTS WITH A VIEW, DOODLEBUG DESIGN, EK SUCCESS, K&COMPANY, KI MEMORIES, LUXE DESIGNS, MAKING MEMORIES, MARVY UCHIDA, ME & MY BIG IDEAS, ORIENTAL TRADING COMPANY, QUEEN &CO., SANDYLION, SCENIC ROUTE AND STAMPIN' UP!

# utensils for the scrapbooking kitchen

**❶** Punches (variety, including basic shapes like circle, square, heart and corner rounder)

**❷** Adhesives (variety of dry, wet and dimensional)

**❸** Scissors (both basic and decorative-edged)

**❹** Ruler

**❺** Paper trimmer

**❻** Paintbrush

**❼** Craft knife

**❽** Self-healing cutting mat

**❾** Paper piercer

**❿** Needle

**⓫** Stapler

BO-BUNNY PRESS, CARL MANUFACTURING, CONTEMPORARY CRAFTS, EK SUCCESS, FIBER SCRAPS, LOEW-CORNELL, MAKING MEMORIES, MCGILL, PAZZLES, SCRAPBOOK ADHESIVES BY 3L, W R MEMORY KEEPERS AND WESTCOTT.

# pantry-only pages

It just can't get any easier than this! You're all ready with the ingredients you need, so tie on an apron and start whipping up these no-fail layouts today.

TOTAL TIME TO SCRAPLIFT:

# 20
## minutes

## from the pantry

- ☐ 5 sheets of cardstock

- ☐ 1 striped chipboard or patterned-paper strip

- ☐ 2 chipboard shapes

- ☐ Several chipboard or foam dots (or brads)

- ☐ 1 set dimensional letter stickers

- ☐ 1 computer font

- ☐ 5 photographs

You order your Jamba Ju_
flavor. "What kind do you _
you always reply, "P _
something with strawber_
more orange than pink. C _
Juices at the Jamba Juice_
then do our grocery sho_
hand. Invariably, halfwa_
section you start saying, _
and then I have to put yo_
When we get into the car _
your drink is and I always_
are not allowed to drink i_
from an experience with y_
around the age you are n_
smelled very fruity for a v_
get home, you finish you_
in your own space and on_

**Jamba Juice** *by Vivian Masket.* **Supplies** *Cardstock:* Bazzill Basics Paper; *Striped chipboard strip:* Scenic Route; *Letter stickers and chipboard shapes:* American Crafts; *Font:* Arial Narrow.

## make it (even) easier!

Replace the four-photo block with a single 4" x 6" print.

# jamba juice

ce by color instead of by
want, Sadie?" I ask, and
ink." I usually order
ies that turns out to be
ops! We buy our Jamba
inside Whole Foods and
pping with our drinks in
y through the produce
"I'm freezing, Mommy!"
r drink down in the cart.
you want to know where
have to explain that you
in the car (this I learned
our brother when he was
w – let's just say our car
ery long time!). When we
drink, happy to enjoy it
your own time.

## INSTRUCTIONS

1 Crop four photos to 2" x 3" to create block. Adhere block to center of left-hand page, and focal-point photo to center of right-hand page. Trim white cardstock and mat layout on pink paper.

2 Type journaling, trim to 4" x 6" and add between photos. Add striped chipboard strip to bottom of photos and journaling.

3 Apply foam letter stickers and dots or brads. Use dimensional adhesive to raise swirl shapes off page.

TOTAL TIME TO SCRAPLIFT:

# 45
## minutes

## from the pantry

- ☐ 3 sheets cardstock (1 scalloped)
- ☐ 2 sheets dot patterned paper
- ☐ 1 set chipboard letter stickers
- ☐ 1 chipboard heart
- ☐ Embroidery floss
- ☐ Stamping ink
- ☐ 1 computer font
- ☐ 4 photographs 4×6

Nothing says summer has arrived like daddy grilling on the BBQ.

The kids favorite (and moms too) is fresh corn on the cob!

Everyone is sure to be happy when it is served up.

MMM nothing beats good summer eats.

**Summer Eats** by Shannon Brouwer. **Supplies** *Cardstock:* Bazzill Basics Paper; *Patterned paper:* Bo-Bunny Press; *Chipboard letters:* Scenic Route; *Chipboard heart:* Heidi Swapp for Advantus; *Embroidery floss:* DMC; *Ink:* ColorBox, Clearsnap; *Font:* High Tide.

## make it (even) easier!

Forego the inking and tearing for
a super-fast alternative.

### INSTRUCTIONS

1   Mat photos on yellow cardstock, but don't trim bottom edge. Tear bottom edge, leaving room for title and journaling. Ink top and sides of cardstock and mount on dot paper.

2   Create journaling on computer, cut into strips and attach to layout. Add scalloped border to bottom edge of photos.

3   Apply chipboard heart and title, adding hand-stitching to a couple of the letters.

TOTAL TIME TO SCRAPLIFT:

## 30 minutes

## from the pantry

- ☐ 1 sheet cardstock

- ☐ 3 sheets patterned paper (striped, scalloped and grid)

- ☐ 3 rub-ons (letters, swirl and circle)

- ☐ 4 sets letter and number stickers (various)

- ☐ 1 chipboard tree

- ☐ 5 photographs

## INSTRUCTIONS

1 Mat cardstock on grid paper. Arrange photos into block, leaving small margins between them. Attach to page.

2 Place small strips of striped paper along left edge and bottom of photos, extending to edge of mat. Add strip of scalloped paper along far left.

3 Create title with various letter stickers. Apply rub-on sentiment, circle and swirl. Finish with date and tree stickers.

## make it (even) easier!
Print your title on a separate piece of cardstock and cut it to fit.

**2 Winter Boys** by Ruth Dealey. **Supplies** *Cardstock:* Bazzill Basics Paper; *Patterned paper, rub-ons, chipboard tree, journaling spot and foam stickers:* American Crafts; *Number stickers:* American Crafts ("2") and Making Memories ("08").

## bonus project

Look how effectively Ruth used the same supplies on a sweet little card!

**Eat Cake** by Ruth Dealey. **Supplies** *Cardstock:* Bazzill Basics Paper (white) and Prism Papers (green); *Patterned paper, rub-ons and ribbon:* American Crafts; *Brads:* Making Memories; *Corner-rounder punch:* EK Success; *Other:* Flower.

## 20
minutes

If, in the future, you have nightmares of being crushed, pressed or smashed...? It may possibly have something to do with me and my daily statement...

You're so cute, I want to

# squish
you to pieces!

7 months

**Squish** by Deena Wuest. **Supplies** *Software:* Adobe Photoshop Elements 4.0; *Digital patterned paper (altered):* Retrophide by Jesse Edwards; *Fonts:* Avant Garde and Steelfish.

## from the pantry

☐  2 sheets cardstock

☐  1 sheet patterned paper (floral)

☐  1 set letter stickers

☐  1 set rub-on letters

☐  1 or 2 computer fonts

☐  1 photograph

## make it
## (even) easier!

Print your title right on the photo
for an even faster finish.

## INSTRUCTIONS

*Although Deena produced this page digitally, you can easily re-create the design using paper and traditional supplies.*

1  Print journaling on cardstock. Find a round object (a plate or platter) and place on cardstock. Use a pencil to trace around the object, cut curved paper segments and attach to layout.

2  Attach photo to left side of dark 4" x 11" cardstock strip.

3  Use rub-ons and letter stickers to add title, age and date.

TOTAL TIME TO SCRAPLIFT:

# 30
## minutes

## from the pantry

- ☐ 2 sheets patterned paper (green and gold)
- ☐ 12 photo corner stickers
- ☐ 1 pen
- ☐ 2 computer fonts
- ☐ 15 photographs

tiger   zebra   snakes   orangutang   lions   hippos

snow leopard cub

metro toronto zoo

**Metro Toronto Zoo** by Christine Stoneman. **Supplies** *Software:* Adobe Photoshop Elements 5.0; *Patterned paper:* BasicGrey; *Photo corners:* Canson; *Pen:* Zig Writer, EK Success; *Fonts:* Tahoma and Times New Roman; *Other:* Circle punch.

## make it (even) easier!

Create a title and additional text by using rub-ons.

flamingo   indian rhino   golden monkey   macaws   ram

*september '07*

Marlene and I decided to take a day of work one Thursday in late November and head down to the Toronto Zoo for a photo safari. It took us forever to get out of Ottawa, with the rush hour and some very heavy rains, but when we arrived at the zoo with our backpacks of camera gear, we were ready to go. It had been at least 15 years since I had been to the zoo, and I found it to be world class as always, with spacious, educational exhibits set in a beautiful ravine setting. We walked and walked and talked and talked and snapped away

having a grand old time. We had a brief lunch and then hit the trails again. I had my cool new telephoto with me and I was quiet pleased with it, it even did well in low light, zoomed in. It would be really hard to pick a favourite animal, but the baby snow leopards were certainly a favourite, and of course the tigers are always stunning. We lingered until closing time and then headed off down the highway back home – when we came to a rest stop we knew we had walked a lot because we sure felt stiff getting out of the car! What a perfect day.

## INSTRUCTIONS

1 Crop small photos to create strip across top of layout.

2 Create word strip, title, tag and journaling on computer. Print and attach. Punch circle out of large photo.

3 Attach large photo to left side of background paper, and three medium photos to right. Add photo corners if desired. Finish with tag and handwritten date.

TOTAL TIME TO SCRAPLIFT:

# 20
## minutes

## from the pantry

- ☐ 2 sheets cardstock
- ☐ 2 sheets patterned paper (striped and dot)
- ☐ 1 set chipboard letter stickers
- ☐ 4 chipboard stars
- ☐ 1 brad
- ☐ 1 computer font
- ☐ 4 photographs 4×6

## make it
## (even) easier!

To save even more time,
handwrite your journaling.

nintendo

Turning nine was mighty fine. One of Nathan's favorite presents was a brand new white Nintendo DS.

**Nintendo** by Michelle St. Clair. **Supplies** *Cardstock:* Bazzill Basics Paper; *Patterned paper:* Tinkering Ink; *Chipboard stars and letter stickers:* American Crafts; *Brad:* Doodlebug Design; *Font:* Tahoma.

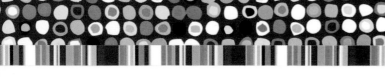

His old Gameboy Advance games are compatible; he also got a few new games: Garfield A Tail of Two Kitties, Nintendogs, Shrek the Third, and Spongebob Square Pants The Yellow Avenger.

## INSTRUCTIONS

1 Line up photos on the lower two-thirds of background cardstock. Use one vertical picture for visual interest. Measure space and type journaling to fit beneath photos.

2 Add three strips of patterned paper in coordinating colors above and beneath the photos. Apply letter stickers for title.

3 Embellish with chipboard stars and brad.

# 20
## minutes

## from the pantry

- ☐ 3 sheets cardstock
- ☐ 2 sets letter stickers
- ☐ 1 set rub-on letters
- ☐ 3 chipboard circles
- ☐ 1 brad
- ☐ 1 pen
- ☐ 1 computer font
- ☐ 3 photographs **4×6**

**Simply Dashing** by Renee Foss. **Supplies** *Cardstock and brad:* Bazzill Basics Paper; *Chipboard circles:* Fancy Pants Designs; *Letter stickers:* Making Memories (large) and Memories Complete (small); *Rub-on letters:* American Crafts; *Pen:* Uni-ball Signo, Newell Rubbermaid; *Font:* Kingthings Printingkit.

## INSTRUCTIONS

1 Create journaling on computer and print. Mat three vertical photos on black cardstock and attach to red background.

2 Cover chipboard with orange cardstock and ink edges with pen. Apply to layout.

3 Form title with letter stickers and use rub-on letters to journal on photo. Finish with brad.

## make it (even) easier!

Don't have a wide-format printer? Print your journaling on a smaller piece of paper and attach it to the background piece.

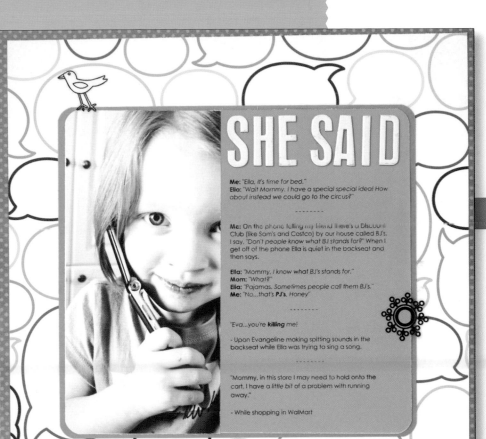

**20 minutes**

## from the pantry

- ☐ 2 sheets cardstock
- ☐ 2 sheets patterned paper (dot and graphic)
- ☐ 1 set chipboard letter stickers
- ☐ 2 clear stickers
- ☐ 1 computer font
- ☐ 1 photograph

**She Said** by Emilie Ahern. **Supplies** *Cardstock:* Bo-Bunny Press and WorldWin; *Patterned paper and stickers:* American Crafts; *Chipboard letters:* Heidi Swapp for Advantus; *Corner-rounder punch:* EK Success; *Font:* Century Gothic.

## make it (even) easier!

Copy your journaling from a blog or journal entry.

## INSTRUCTIONS

1 Type and print journaling. Round the outer corners of photo and photo mat. Mat journaling and photo together on cardstock.

2 Trim and mat large patterned paper on smaller patterned paper. Attach photo mat on top.

3 Apply chipboard letters and small stickers to finish.

TOTAL TIME TO SCRAPLIFT:

# 20
## minutes

☐ 3 sheets cardstock

☐ 2 sheets patterned paper
(floral and striped)

☐ 1 set letter stickers

☐ 2 phrase stickers

☐ 1 computer font

☐ 6 photographs 4×6

**Already?** by Stephanie Vetne. **Supplies** *Cardstock:* Bazzill Basics Paper; *Patterned paper and letter stickers:* SEI; *Phrase stickers:* 7gypsies; *Font:* Garamond.

## make it (even) easier!

A strip of handwritten
journaling will save
even more time.

she's only 9!

i'm ready for my close up

thing, but not me. I showed her how to put her hair up, make the water lukewarm, lather up her face, and rinse off in the sink. Oh. It was sinking in bit by bit as I was watching her. She was very thorough and not at all put off by this new chore she suddenly was going to have to do every night for the rest of her life. She was now thoroughly delighted with the whole thing and kept asking if I thought she was really getting pimples. Like it was an exciting event! Um… yes, honey, you do have a blemish, but I guess you're now considered a pre-teen and we'll just keep working on keeping your face clean. And your mother's heart from panicking. (2007)

## INSTRUCTIONS

1 Mat six photos on striped patterned paper, trim and attach toward bottom of black cardstock background.

2 Create journaling strips on computer. Attach to layout and add punched floral patterned-paper circles.

3 Add phrase stickers to photos. Finish with letter stickers for title.

TOTAL TIME TO SCRAPLIFT:

# 45
minutes

☐ 5 sheets cardstock
(1 scalloped)

☐ 2 sheets patterned paper (dot)

☐ 1 yard ribbon

☐ 1 set chipboard letters

☐ 16 brads

☐ 1 journaling stamp

☐ 1 inkpad

☐ 2 pens (black and white)

☐ 7 photographs 4×6

## INSTRUCTIONS

1 Trim and mat tan cardstock on dot paper. Place
vertical photos on bottom and horizontal photos on
top of layout, leaving room for title and journaling.
Attach strip of scalloped cardstock across middle of
page and embellish with ribbon and brads.

2 Hand cut mouse ears out of cardstock. Attach to
layout and top with glittered chipboard letters.
Accent red punched stars with white pen. Layer with
black punched stars and add to page.

3 Stamp journaling lines and write journaling with pen.

**Disney** by Lisa Dorsey. **Supplies** *Cardstock:* Bazzill Basics Paper (white scalloped), Die Cuts With a View (black) and WorldWin (tan); *Patterned paper:* Bo-Bunny Press; *Chipboard letters and ribbon:* Making Memories; *Stamp:* gel-à-tins; *Ink:* Clearsnap; *Star punch:* Marvy Uchida; *Brads:* Creative Imaginations; *Pens:* Zig Writer, EK Success; Sharpie, Newell Rubbermaid.

## make it
## (even) easier!

Use premade star
accents for a quick finish.

Great rides

It's a Small World

Those goofy Pirates

It is virtually impossible to see all of Disney in one visit but we definitely tried. We had each day planned out so we could make the most of our trip. We had such a wonderful time. We would love to go back again soon. Maybe next time we'll stay 2 weeks!

Miss U

## bonus project

Follow Lisa's lead and use your scraps to create a cute card!

**Miss U** by Lisa Dorsey. **Supplies** *Cardstock:* Bazzill Basics Paper (white scalloped), Die Cuts With a View (black) and WorldWin (tan); *Patterned paper:* Bo-Bunny Press; *Chipboard letters:* Making Memories; *Letter stickers:* Arctic Frog.

TOTAL TIME TO SCRAPLIFT:

# 30
minutes

- ☐ 2 sheets cardstock
- ☐ 1 sheet patterned paper
- ☐ 2 sets letter stickers
- ☐ 3 sticker accents
- ☐ 2 sets rub-ons
- ☐ 1 computer font
- ☐ 7 photographs

**Beautiful Sunday** by Paula Gilarde. **Supplies** *Cardstock:* Stampin' Up!; *Patterned paper:* Bo-Bunny Press; *Stickers:* Scrapworks; *Rub-ons:* BasicGrey (white) and Hambly Screen Prints (green); *Corner-rounder punch:* EK Success; *Font:* Trebuchet MS.

## make it
(even) easier!

Replace the rub-ons
with clear stickers.

Weather-wise, it was not a good Sunday. It was grey and overcast with a little mist. Definitely not a typical beach day, or even a good day for sight seeing. But you do what you can when you are on vacation in Ireland and so we put on our rain-boots, and zipped up our jackets and headed out for a walk. Without the sun, our walk along the water's edge was a totally different experience, and gave us the change to explore all kinds of things that we had previously missed like the caves in Sladeen and all those strange markings in the sand. The tower at Loch looked mysterious and eerie in the fog. The kids were so distracted that they didn't even notice how far we walked - we went from Loch, to the lighthouse, along to cliffs to Beenban and back to the house again! In fact, as far as we were concerned it was a...

beautiful SUNDAY

## INSTRUCTIONS

1 Type and print journaling on patterned paper and trim to 4" wide. Arrange photos and journaling block on page, leaving small margins between them. Round the four outer corners and attach to cardstock.

2 Apply rub-ons to edges of design.

3 Add title letters, allowing them to overlap onto photo and cardstock.

## 30 minutes

### from the pantry

- ☐ 1 sheet cardstock
- ☐ 1 sheet patterned paper (dot)
- ☐ 2 sets dimensional letter stickers
- ☐ 2 photo corner stickers
- ☐ 2 computer fonts
- ☐ 7 photographs (or sheet of school photos)

It's been a rough first quarter. Administrative authoritarianism. Piles of papers. Daily demands. Stress, stress, stress. To be honest, there have been days I just wanted to call it quits. But then came parent/teacher conferences. Some teachers approach these conferences with anxiety and apprehension, but for me it was exactly what I needed. Finally I heard what I'd been so badly in need of hearing — positive comments and lots of them!

## phrases I want to remember from

# parent/teacher conferences

"Erin adores you! She says she's learned more so far this year in English than any other year!"

"Craig shared with me that you are his favorite teacher, and he wanted me to tell you."

"Amanda loves how organized and color coordinated you are! She says that everything matches."

"Joel knows that you care about how he does."

"Molly's confidence in writing comes from your encouragement."

"Tom is glad to have you again this year."

"Abby feels so comfortable with you."

"Kenny enjoys your class so much!"

2007-08

**Parent-Teacher Conferences** by Susan Opel. **Supplies** *Cardstock:* Bazzill Basics Paper; *Patterned paper:* Creative Imaginations; *Stickers:* American Crafts (black letters) and Creative Imaginations (red epoxy letters and corners); *Fonts:* Century Gothic (title) and Olympus (journaling).

### INSTRUCTIONS

1 Print journaling on cardstock, leaving room for title. Apply photo strip from school pictures on an angle. Trim off excess.

2 Add computer-generated word strip and letter stickers for title.

3 Apply patterned paper and photo corners to finish.

## make it (even) easier!

If the slanted journaling seems too overwhelming, just arrange the pictures straight up and down.

**Smile** by Emilie Ahern. **Supplies** *Cardstock:* WorldWin; *Patterned paper and letter stickers:* October Afternoon; *Chipboard accents and word-strip paper:* Scenic Route; *Pen:* Zig Millennium, EK Success.

TOTAL TIME TO SCRAPLIFT:

## 20 minutes

### from the pantry

- ☐ 1 sheet cardstock
- ☐ 5 patterned papers (dot, orange, grid, lined and word)
- ☐ 1 chipboard accent
- ☐ 1 sheet letter stickers
- ☐ 1 pen
- ☐ 1 photograph 4×6

## make it (even) easier!

Use a premade circle accent to make this design even simpler.

## INSTRUCTIONS

1 Apply strip of dot paper to cardstock. Cut patterned paper in a circle and place under left-bottom corner of photo. Attach both atop dot paper.

2 Add word strip and grid paper piece under photo. Hand cut scalloped edge on small piece of lined patterned paper and apply beneath grid paper. Write journaling on larger piece.

3 Complete with chipboard accent and title.

TOTAL TIME TO SCRAPLIFT:

0
15
30
45

## 20
minutes

- ☐ 2 sheets cardstock
  (1 laser-edged)

- ☐ 2 sheets patterned paper

- ☐ 2 sets chipboard letters

- ☐ 3 large brads

- ☐ 1 inkpad

- ☐ 1 computer font

- ☐ 5 photographs

**Feeding the Reindeer** by Julie Detlef. **Supplies** *Cardstock:* Bazzill Basics Paper; *Patterned paper and laser-cut paper:* TaDa Creative Studios; *Chipboard letters:* American Crafts; *Brads:* Creative Impressions; *Ink:* ColorBox, Clearsnap; *Font:* Kids Scrawl.

## make it
## (even) easier!

Eliminate laser-edged
cardstock and use other
accents instead.

he reindeer

We started a tradition at our new house last year. Each year after we frost and decorate our Christmas cut-out cookies we save all the extra colored sugar. Then we add oatmeal and mix them together. We call this mixture "treats for the reindeer." On Christmas Eve, Sydnee takes the mixture out and spreads it around so the reindeer will have a treat when they stop by the house. Sydnee always remembers to spread a little more where she thinks Rudolph will be landing. I love this new tradition, and I can't wait until Shay is old enough to join her.

## INSTRUCTIONS

1 Mat photos on laser-edged paper, trimming the edge to allow room for title. Attach to background paper.

2 Ink edges of chipboard letters. Apply to layout.

3 Type journaling, changing font color of key words as desired. Attach journaling to layout with large brads.

TOTAL TIME TO SCRAPLIFT:

## 30 minutes

### from the pantry

- ☐ 3 sheets cardstock
- ☐ 5 patterned papers (dot, red text, blue text, yellow and orange)
- ☐ 4 epoxy stickers
- ☐ 1 set letter stickers
- ☐ 1 pen
- ☐ 4 photographs 4×6

## make it (even) easier!

Ribbon or a border strip make for a cool edge without the need for decorative-edged scissors.

**Olympic Park** by Kelly Purkey. **Supplies** *Cardstock and pen:* American Crafts; *Patterned paper:* American Crafts (green dot), Doodlebug Design (red text), Heidi Swapp for Advantus (yellow, orange) and KI Memories (blue letter); *Epoxy stickers:* Cloud 9 Design, Fiskars; *Letter stickers:* Heidi Grace Designs; *Decorative-edged scissors:* Fiskars; *Other:* Star punch and pen.

## INSTRUCTIONS

1 Attach red patterned paper to black cardstock and accent with strips of other papers (trim one with decorative-edged scissors). Place three vertical photos on red paper and fill space between with yellow patterned paper.

2 Mat focal-point photo on yellow paper. Add handwritten journaling and letter stickers for title. Mount on layout with dimensional adhesive dots.

3 Embellish punched stars with epoxy stickers and add to layout.

TOTAL TIME TO SCRAPLIFT:

0
15
30
45

## 30
minutes

## from the pantry

☐ 2 sheets cardstock

☐ 2 sheets patterned paper
(striped and plaid)

☐ 2 sets letter stickers

☐ 2 chipboard accents

☐ 1 computer font

☐ 6 photographs

When we saw the ad in the newspaper for the Traveling Zoo we knew that we should go. Not because of the animals, but because of the fair. It had been months since we last got to go on rides. Molly agreed to go if there weren't any goats - only to find out that there were more goats there than all the other animals combined! The rides more than made up for it though - she loved them all. She even went on an elephant! Tommy was unimpressed by the rides (as usual). I think that the unicow was the only thing that he liked!

**Traveling Zoo** by Paula Gilarde. **Supplies** *Cardstock:* Bazzill Basics Paper; *Patterned paper:* October Afternoon; *Letter stickers:* American Crafts; *Chipboard letters:* Scenic Route; *Chipboard accents:* Junkitz (circle) and Technique Tuesday (star); *Font:* Century Gothic.

## make it
## (even) easier!

Paint the star or use a
premade accent.

## INSTRUCTIONS

1 Print journaling on background cardstock. Attach photos in a grouping, making sure to keep edges aligned.

2 Tear edges of plaid paper and add to layout. Cover chipboard star with striped paper. Cut strip and punch circle out of striped paper. Attach all to layout.

3 Add chipboard word circle around star and use letter stickers to create title.

# 30
## minutes

## from the pantry

- ☐ 2 sheets cardstock
- ☐ 2 sheets patterned paper (red and cream)
- ☐ 1 set letter stickers
- ☐ 5 stickers (tabs and stars)
- ☐ 2 inkpads
- ☐ 1 pen
- ☐ 3 photographs 4×6

**Battery Park** by Mou Saha. **Supplies** *Cardstock:* Frances Meyer; *Patterned paper, stickers and tabs:* Rusty Pickle; *Ink:* Tsukineko; *Pen:* American Crafts.

## INSTRUCTIONS

1 Write journaling on notebook paper. Mat two photos and journaling on patterned papers and attach to layout.

2 Add third photo and strip of patterned paper on left page. Ink and journal on tabs and add to edges of papers.

3 Accent layout with inked star stickers. Ink letters and apply title.

## make it (even) easier!

Leave off the tabs and you'll be done even sooner!

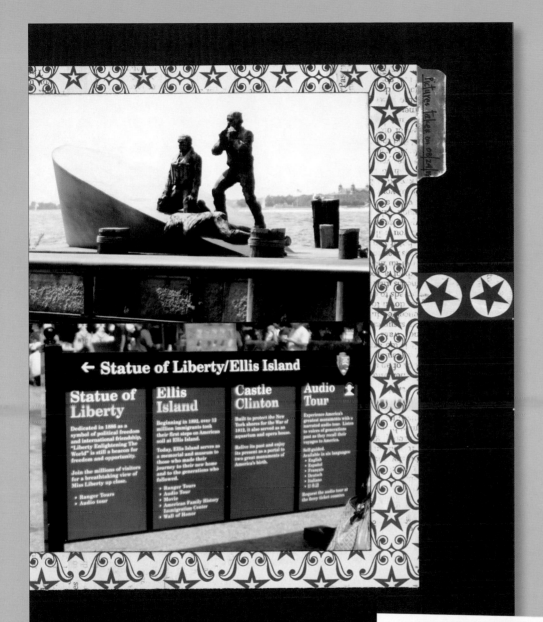

← **Statue of Liberty/Ellis Island**

**Statue of Liberty**

Dedicated in 1886 as a symbol of political freedom and international friendship, "Liberty Enlightening The World" is still a beacon for freedom and opportunity.

Join the millions of visitors for a breathtaking view of Miss Liberty up close.

- Ranger Tours
- Audio tour

**Ellis Island**

Beginning in 1892, over 12 million immigrants took their first steps on American soil at Ellis Island.

Today, Ellis Island serves as a memorial and museum to those who made their journey to their new home and to the generations who followed.

- Ranger Tours
- Audio Tour
- Movie
- American Family History
- Immigration Center
- Wall of Honor

**Castle Clinton**

Built to protect the New York shores for the War of 1812, it also served as an aquarium and opera house.

Relive its past and enjoy its present as a portal to two great monuments of America's birth.

**Audio Tour**

Experience America's greatest monuments with a narrated audio tour. Listen to voices of generations past as they recall their steps to America.

Self-guided. Available in six languages:
- English
- Español
- Français
- Deutsch
- Italiano
- 日本語

Repeat the audio tour at the ferry ticket counter.

## bonus project

While you've got your supplies out, use the extras to create this trendy card.

**Thanks** by Mou Saha. **Supplies** *Cardstock:* Frances Meyer; *Patterned paper, stickers and tabs:* Rusty Pickle; *Ink:* Tsukineko; *Pre-folded card:* Halcraft USA; *Pen:* American Crafts.

TOTAL TIME TO SCRAPLIFT:

## 20 minutes

from the pantry

- ☐ 3 sheets cardstock
- ☐ 1 sheet patterned paper
- ☐ 1 sheet rub-on letters
- ☐ 1 set letter stickers
- ☐ 1 sticker (scalloped)
- ☐ 5 chipboard accents
- ☐ 1 brad
- ☐ 1 adhesive badge
- ☐ Embroidery floss
- ☐ 2 photographs  4×6

## make it (even) easier!

Kristina used a punch to create the scalloped border, but you can easily substitute ribbon or a border sticker.

**Always Happy** by Kristina Proffitt. **Supplies** *Cardstock:* The Paper Company; *Patterned paper, chipboard accents, rub-ons, brad, adhesive badge and letter stickers:* American Crafts; *Scallop punch:* Fiskars; *Heart punch:* EK Success; *Other:* Embroidery floss.

## INSTRUCTIONS

1 Center two photos in middle of layout on cardstock. Place strip of patterned paper and scalloped border beneath them.

2 Sew on chipboard star "buttons" and attach chipboard accents. Add adhesive badge and brad.

3 Create title with rub-ons, letter stickers and a scalloped sticker.

# 1
## hour

### from the pantry

☐   5 sheets cardstock

☐   16 brads

☐   Embroidery floss

☐   2 computer fonts

☐   12 photographs

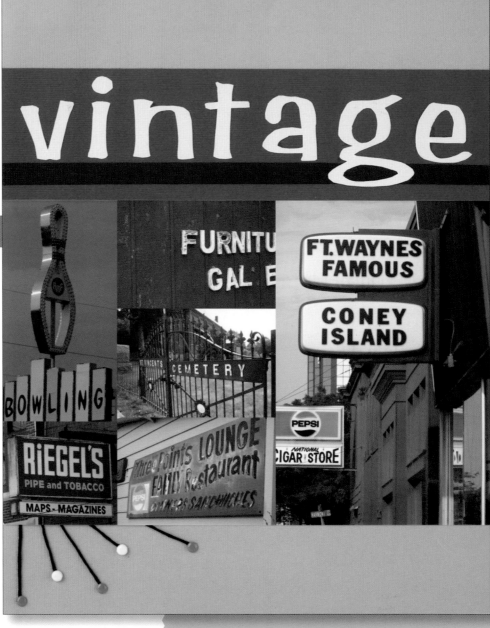

**Vintage Fort Wayne** by Susan Opel. **Supplies** *Cardstock:* Bazzill Basics
Paper (teal, yellow) and Prism Papers (aqua); *Circle punch:* EK Success;
*Brads:* Creative Impressions; *Embroidery floss:* Making Memories; *Fonts:*
Arial Narrow ("Fort Wayne") and Simpson ("Vintage" and journaling).

## make it
## (even) easier!

A letter-sticker title
and rays drawn with pen
save lots of time!

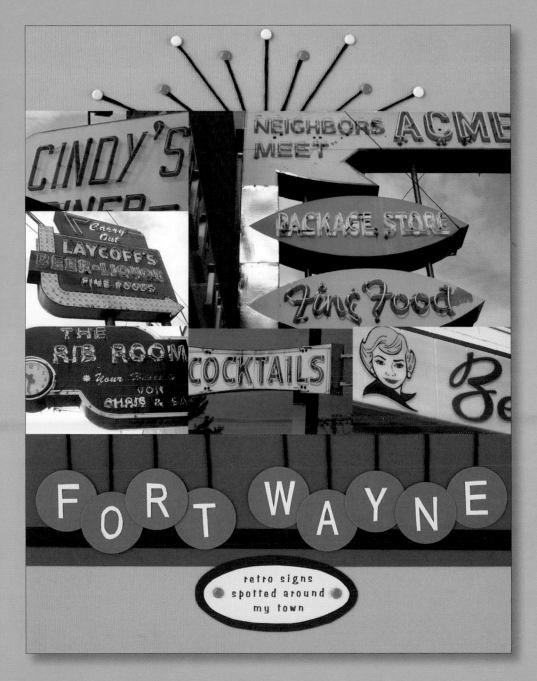

## INSTRUCTIONS

1. Create two 8½" x 6" photo collages. Add teal cardstock section above left-page collage and beneath right-page collage. Accent teal sections with black strips. Apply to aqua background paper.

2. Use computer to create title and journaling. Hand cut letters. Affix title to left side. Punch circles and add letters. Attach to right side of layout with foam tape.

3. Sew "rays" with embroidery floss. Mat journaling on oval. Add brads to rays and tag.

## 20 minutes

### from the pantry

- ☐ 3 sheets cardstock
- ☐ 1 sheet patterned paper (dot)
- ☐ 1 rub-on
- ☐ 13 brads
- ☐ 1 computer font
- ☐ 1 photograph **4×6**

# Bread As Art

I refused to pay $19.95 for a loaf of bread, but I was quite happy to admire the bakers' handiwork. San Francisco, June 2007

the Good Stuff

**Bread as Art** by Vivian Masket. **Supplies** *Cardstock:* Bazzill Basics Paper; *Patterned paper and rub-on:* October Afternoon; *Brads:* American Crafts; *Circle punches:* EK Success; *Dimensional adhesive dot:* Plaid Enterprises; *Font:* AM Sans.

## INSTRUCTIONS

1 Print title and journaling on white cardstock, leaving room between for photo.

2 Trim and mat white cardstock on black background. Tear a strip of patterned paper and adhere to right side of page. Punch half-circle out of photo. Adhere photo to layout.

3 Apply rub-on to punched cardstock circle. Add to punched out portion of photo and embellish dot paper with black brads.

## make it (even) easier!

Color black dots with ink and save the brads for another project.

## 45
minutes

**New Friends** by Kelly Noel. **Supplies** *Software:* Adobe Photoshop Elements 3.0; *Cardstock:* Bazzill Basics Paper; *Patterned paper, laser-cut paper, letter stickers, ribbon, brads and soft embellishments:* KI Memories; *Punches:* Fiskars; *Pen:* Inkessentials, Design Originals; *Font:* Kayleigh.

## from the pantry

☐  3 sheets cardstock
   (1 laser-cut)

☐  5 patterned papers (stripe,
   orange, yellow, pink and blue)

☐  2 sets letter stickers

☐  3 brads

☐  ½ yard ribbon

☐  3 foam stickers

☐  1 pen

☐  1 computer font

☐  1 photograph  4×6

### INSTRUCTIONS

1 Print journaling directly onto photo. Round edges of photo and yellow patterned paper, and attach both to blue flower paper. Apply striped paper strips to top and bottom. Trim and mat on black cardstock and round bottom edge of black mat. Trim and attach all to blue cardstock.

2 Punch hearts in various sizes and colors. Draw "stitching" around edges with pen. Arrange to create flower shapes and top with stickers. Adhere to layout along line of laser-cut paper.

3 Finish with ribbon, colorful letter stickers and brads.

## make it (even) easier!

Write directly on your photo with a white pen.

TOTAL TIME TO SCRAPLIFT:

1
hour

## from the pantry

☐ 3 sheets cardstock

☐ 2 sheets patterned paper

☐ 1 chipboard tag

☐ 2 sets letter stickers

☐ 6 sticker accents
(circles and leaves)

☐ 1 pen

☐ 1 computer font

☐ 5 photographs 4×6

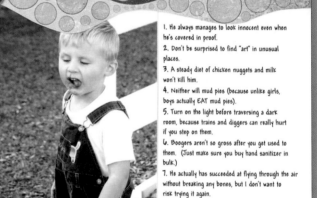

**8 Things I've Learned as Allen's Mom** by Sabrina Ropp. **Supplies** *Cardstock:* Bazzill Basics Paper (green) and *Hobby Lobby* (tan); *Patterned paper:* BasicGrey (waves) and My Mind's Eye (flourishes); *Chipboard tag:* KI Memories; *Stickers:* American Crafts (letters and numbers), BasicGrey (circles) and We R Memory Keepers (leaves); *Pen:* Uni-ball Signo, Newell Rubbermaid; *Font:* Andy.

## make it (even) easier!

Format your journaling to
4" x 6" and have it
printed by your local
photo developer with
your photos.

Sept. 8th 2008

6    7    8

learned as Allen's MOM

## INSTRUCTIONS

1 Type journaling on computer, print and cut to 4" x 6". Arrange photos across middle of layout with journaling card substituting for one photo.

2 Hand-cut wavy strips from patterned paper and apply to top edge of photos. Attach strip of second patterned paper beneath photos. Add number stickers on photos.

3 Combine chipboard tag and letter stickers on brown cardstock to create title. Add sticker. Apply to layout. Finish with handwritten items.

TOTAL TIME TO SCRAPLIFT:

# 1
## hour

## from the pantry

- ☐ 3 sheets cardstock
- ☐ 2 sheets patterned paper (word and striped)
- ☐ 1 set letter stickers
- ☐ 1 set themed stickers
- ☐ 1 inkpad
- ☐ 1 pen
- ☐ 5 photographs

my
hunny

HUNNY

12.01.06 Almost 3 months

**My Hunny** by Leah LaMontagne. **Supplies** *Cardstock: Die Cuts With a View; Patterned paper: Die Cuts With a View (baby blue) and SEI (orange stripe); 3-D stickers: Jolee's Boutique, EK Success; Letter stickers: Arctic Frog; Pen: Zig Writer, EK Success; Other: Ink.*

## make it
## (even) easier!

Save time by adding a
straight journaling strip
instead of a wave.

My favorite things about these pictures of Levi, are his so sweet smiles & that super soft bear-ear baby cap. Even though he has been sick for quite a while (see the red circles under his eyes) . . . He is still so happy & sweet as Hunny!

## INSTRUCTIONS

1 Mat large photo on white cardstock. Mat again on striped paper. Ink edges and mat again on word patterned paper. Use a cup to trace round edges and cut. Apply to left side of layout.

2 Arrange four photos in block on right side of layout. Cut strips of word and striped paper and trace around cup to round outer edges. Add to top left and bottom right of photo block.

3 Hand-cut a wave for journaling strip. Add journaling and cardstock circle to layout. Finish with letter stickers and theme embellishments.

## 20
minutes

### from the pantry

- ☐ 2 sheets cardstock
- ☐ 4 sticker accents
- ☐ 1 set letter stickers
- ☐ 1 pen
- ☐ 4 photographs

*pictures taken on: Sep 02 '08*
RECORDED : SEP 11 '08

**Your Creative Process** by Mou Saha. **Supplies** *Cardstock:* Die Cuts With a View; *Letter stickers:* Luxe Designs; *Crayon stickers:* Frances Meyer; *Pen:* American Crafts.

### INSTRUCTIONS

1 Crop photos into squares and center on two-page layout. Use ruler and pen to draw gridlines between them.

2 Draw additional lines for journaling. Write journaling.

3 Add themed stickers and title letter stickers to finish.

## make it (even) easier!
**Use four uncropped
4" x 6" photos.**

your creative process

Yellow

PICK A PAPER. CHOOSE A COLOR.
THINK... THINK... THINK...
THEN START CREATING A LITTLE
MASTERPIECE. OM, I JUST LOVE
WATCHING YOU CREATE !

## bonus project

**Use the same products to produce this cute greeting card.**

**Create Art Every Day** by Mou Saha.
**Supplies** *Cardstock:* Die Cuts With a
View; *Letter stickers and label stickers:*
Luxe Designs; *Crayon stickers:* Frances
Meyer; *Pre-folded card:* Halcraft USA; *Pen:*
American Crafts.

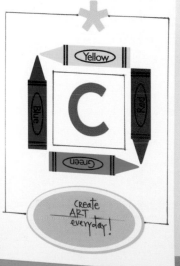

## 45
minutes

### from the pantry

- ☐ 2 sheets cardstock
- ☐ 4 sheets patterned paper (dot, diamond, ledger and cupcake)
- ☐ 1 set letter stickers
- ☐ 2 brads
- ☐ 1 word stamp
- ☐ 1 inkpad
- ☐ 5 chipboard accents
- ☐ 1 pen
- ☐ 4 photographs 4×6

## make it (even) easier!

No decorative-edged scissors? Try a paper with a scalloped edge instead.

**Citizen Cupcake** by Kelly Purkey. **Supplies** *Cardstock:* Bazzill Basics Paper; *Patterned paper:* American Crafts (pink dot), Heidi Grace Designs (blue diamond and cupcake) and Making Memories (ledger); *Letter stickers:* Doodlebug Design; *Chipboard accents:* Heidi Grace Designs; *Decorative-edge scissors:* Fiskars; *Stamp:* Hero Arts; *Ink:* Stampin' Up!; *Brads and pen:* American Crafts.

## INSTRUCTIONS

1. Position four horizontal photos on background cardstock. Add strips of patterned paper along top and bottom of layout, and a block to the right of bottom row of photos.

2. Use decorative-edged scissors to create scalloped border strip. Attach small strips of patterned paper and title to right side of layout.

3. Journal on ledger paper and apply to layout. Stamp word and cut out. Apply to layout with chipboard accents and brads.

TOTAL TIME TO SCRAPLIFT:

# 30
## minutes

The Fun Starts Here by Barb Wong. **Supplies** *Cardstock:* Bazzill Basics Paper; *Patterned paper, chipboard accents and letter stickers:* Scenic Route; *Paint:* Plaid Enterprises; *Ink:* VersaColor, Tsukineko; *Pen:* Uni-ball Signo, Newell Rubbermaid.

## from the pantry

- ☐ 2 sheets cardstock
- ☐ 1 sheet striped patterned paper
- ☐ 1 set letter stickers
- ☐ 4 chipboard accents
- ☐ 1 tube paint
- ☐ 1 inkpad
- ☐ 1 pen
- ☐ 11 photographs

## make it (even) easier!

Use a square punch to get even more photos on your page.

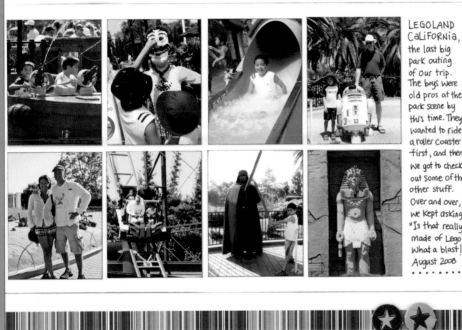

LEGOLAND CALIFORNIA, the last big park outing of our trip. The boys were old pros at the park scene by this time. They wanted to ride a roller coaster first, and then we got to check out some of the other stuff. Over and over, we kept asking, "Is that really made of Lego?" What a blast! August 2008

## INSTRUCTIONS

1   Paint raw chipboard arrow and let dry

2   Crop 10 photos into small rectangles. Ink edges of all photos, including large focal-point photo. Attach to cardstock.

3   Add strip of striped paper along bottom edge of layout, dressing it up with chipboard stickers. Write journaling and add lines with pen and complete with title and arrow.

TOTAL TIME TO SCRAPLIFT:

## 30 minutes

### from the pantry

☐ 3 sheets cardstock
   (1 laser-cut)

☐ 2 sheets patterned paper
   (dot and circles)

☐ 1 journaling stamp

☐ 1 inkpad

☐ 1 set rub-on letters

☐ 1 pen

☐ 4 photographs **4×6**

**Coaching the Inferno** by Sharon Miller. **Supplies** *Cardstock:* Bazzill Basics Paper; *Patterned paper and lace paper:* KI Memories; *Rub-on letters:* Scrapworks; *Journaling stamp:* Autumn Leaves; *Ink:* VersaFine, Tsukineko; *Pen:* American Crafts.

### INSTRUCTIONS

1. Stamp with journaling stamp in a vertical line along right side of two-page layout. Attach three horizontal photos in a line near bottom of layout, covering portion of stamping. Add vertical focal-point photo to top left of right page.

2. Apply red dot paper to top two-thirds of left side. Cover a portion with laser-cut number paper, and the remainder with a strip of coordinating patterned paper.

3. Handwrite journaling and add rub-on letters for title.

## make it (even) easier!

Use a bold patterned paper in place of the laser-cut paper.

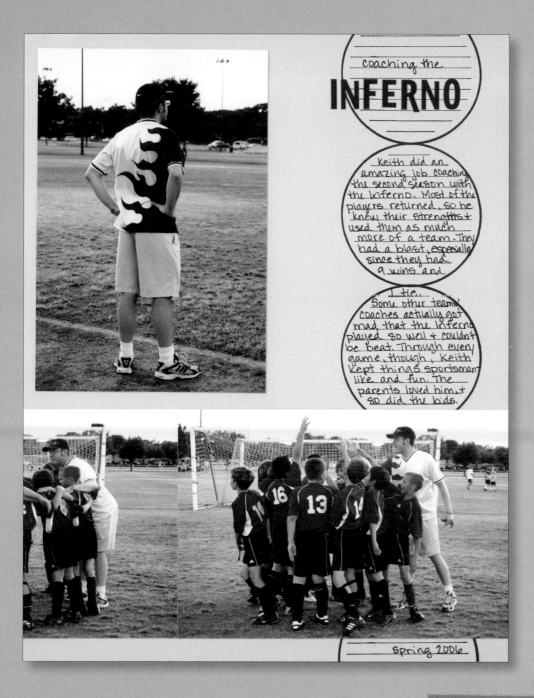

coaching the
# INFERNO

Keith did an amazing job coaching the second season with the Inferno. Most of the players returned, so he knew their strengths + used them as much more of a team. They had a blast, especially since they had 9 wins and

1 tie. Some other teams' coaches actually got mad that the Inferno played so well + couldn't be beat. Through every game, though, Keith kept things sportsmanlike and fun. The parents loved him, + so did the kids.

Spring 2006

## bonus project

Before she cleaned off her stamp, Sharon used it (and other scraps from her layout) to assemble this striking card.

**Happy Birthday 27** by Sharon Miller.
**Supplies** *Cardstock:* Bazzill Basics Paper; *Patterned paper:* KI Memories; *Rub-on sentiment:* Making Memories; *Journaling stamp:* Autumn Leaves; *Ink:* VersaFine, Tsukineko; *Adhesive:* Pioneer.

## 20
minutes

### from the pantry

- ☐ 1 sheet cardstock
- ☐ 1 sheet patterned paper (blue)
- ☐ 1 set rub-on letters
- ☐ Thread
- ☐ 1 pen
- ☐ 5 photographs

new london to orient point. 8.4.05 ...

so much to see.

The fERRy

**The Ferry** by Judith Mara. **Supplies** *Cardstock:* Bazzill Basics Paper; *Patterned paper:* Lazar StudioWerx; *Rub-ons:* Doodlebug Design; *Pen:* Zig Millennium, EK Success; *Other:* Thread.

### INSTRUCTIONS

1. Arrange photos in a grid, leaving equal amounts of space between each.

2. Cut strips and waves out of patterned paper. Stitch to layout

3. Add rub-ons for title, and journal along waves with pen.

## make it (even) easier!

Skip the stitching and simply attach the patterned paper with adhesive.

30
minutes

**Uniquely You** by Laina Lamb. **Supplies** *Cardstock:* Bazzill Basics Paper (white) and WorldWin (blue); *Patterned paper:* KI Memories; *Stitched ribbon and letter stickers:* American Crafts; *Chipboard circles:* Bazzill Basics Paper; *Brads:* Making Memories; *Punches:* EK Success for Stampin' Up!; *Other:* Foam adhesive dots.

## make it (even) easier!

Use rub-ons or write your journaling directly on the photo.

**from the pantry**

- ☐ 14 sheets cardstock (or scraps)
- ☐ 2 sheets patterned paper (floral and striped)
- ☐ 2 sets letter stickers
- ☐ 1 sticker (arrow)
- ☐ 6 chipboard circles
- ☐ ½ yard ribbon
- ☐ 6 brads
- ☐ 1 computer font
- ☐ 3 photographs

## INSTRUCTIONS

1 Cut 11" x 11" square of white cardstock and round corners. Mat in center of blue cardstock. Use computer to journal on photo. Print photos and attach to white cardstock.

2 Add ribbon and strip of striped paper. Cover chipboard circles with various cardstock colors. Cut flowers out of patterned paper and attach to chipboard circles with foam dots. Attach to layout with brads.

3 Add stickers for title. Finish with arrow embellishment.

TOTAL TIME TO SCRAPLIFT:

## 20 minutes

### from the pantry

☐  2 sheets cardstock

☐  2 sheets patterned paper

☐  1 set letter stickers

☐  3 label stickers

☐  1 heart sticker

☐  1 pen

☐  3 photographs **4×6**

We Love Lobster Rolls by Vivian Masket. **Supplies** *Cardstock:* Bazzill Basics Paper; *Patterned paper and label stickers:* Jenni Bowlin Studio; *Letter stickers:* Doodlebug Design; *Star punch:* Fiskars; *Dimensional adhesive:* Plaid Enterprises; *Pen:* American Crafts.

## make it (even) easier!

With premade star embellishments, this layout will practically assemble itself!

## INSTRUCTIONS

1. Attach three vertical photos in center of two-page background. They should be slightly closer to the bottom of the layout. Add sections of patterned paper to each side of photo block.

2. Apply letter stickers for title. Add label stickers and write journaling.

3. Punch stars and adhere with dimensional adhesive. Hand draw line around edge of design.

# 30
## minutes

## from the pantry

☐ 2 sheets cardstock

☐ 4 sheets patterned paper
(word, scalloped and
2 striped)

☐ 1 set letter stickers

☐ 3 chipboard stars

☐ 14 brads

☐ 1 computer font

☐ 7 photographs

**Spirit** by Courtney Kelly. **Supplies** *Cardstock:* Bazzill Basics Paper; *Patterned paper:* Creative Imaginations (scalloped) and KI Memories (striped and word); *Letter stickers:* Making Memories; *Chipboard stars:* American Crafts; *Font:* Book Antiqua; *Other:* Brads and corner-rounder punch.

## make it
## (even) easier!

Leaving the corners square
will save a step.

It doesn't take much to get us going; my family has always been known to put the "fun" in dysfunction, what can I say, we've got spirit. But this particular time it was called for. We are good friends with the GM for the Glacier Pilots Baseball Team and every time he does a themed game we come out and show our support. In addition to St. Patty's, country night, Military day, and of course the 4th of July games, we came out for Halloween in June. Along with maybe the 7 other people who got the memo. But that's okay; Kris and I seized the opportunity for an impromptu photo shoot at the ballpark.

# Spirit

JUNE 13, 2008

## INSTRUCTIONS

1 Crop several photos to make a grouping and mat with subtle striped paper. Add strips of various patterned papers to left and right of photo block, rounding corners of far left strip.

2 Type journaling, trim and attach to layout. Create title with letter stickers.

3 Place scalloped strip along edge of large photo and add brads. Embellish with chipboard stars.

TOTAL TIME TO SCRAPLIFT:

## 20 minutes

**Butterflies of Costa Rica** by Lisa Brown Caveney
**Supplies** *Textured cardstock:* Prism Papers; *Other:* Letter stickers.

OF COSTA RICA

## INSTRUCTIONS

1 Cut an orange strip of cardstock and attach it across the middle of the layout.

2 Apply white letter stickers to the orange strip. *Variation:* For extra visual interest, place small scraps of peach cardstock underneath the letter centers before you adhere the stickers to the orange strip.

3 Crop eight photos into squares and attach them to your layout, arranging four above and four below the orange title strip.

TOTAL TIME TO SCRAPLIFT:

## 30 minutes

☐ 2 sheets of cardstock

☐ 2 sheets of patterned paper (striped)

☐ 1 sheet of rub-on letters

☐ 1 set of letter stamps

☐ 1 inkpad

☐ 1 pen

☐ 6 photographs

**Daddy's Costume** by Shannon Taylor
**Supplies** *Patterned paper:* Rusty Pickle; *Rub-ons:* K&Company; *Pen:* Zig Writer, EK Success; *Other:* Letter stamps and stamping ink.

**Daddy's Costume**

What a TREASURE! While sifting thru her things, Becky came across this sweet little DOG costume that she made for your Daddy when he was little. There are days I can't even get you out of it. MY plan is TO save it for my grandchildren.

## INSTRUCTIONS

1 Mat your photos on two strips of card-stock. Adhere each strip to a piece of patterned paper.

2 On a separate sheet of cardstock, apply rub-on letters to create your title.

3 Handwrite your journaling, leaving spaces for stamped words. To make the stamped words pop, stamp the letters on patterned paper and mat each one with cardstock.

TOTAL TIME TO SCRAPLIFT:

# 30
## minutes

## from the pantry

☐ 2 sheets of cardstock

☐ 3 strips of patterned paper
(floral, striped and geometric)

☐ 3-6 sheets of letter stickers
(*Tip:* Mix and match
various leftovers.)

☐ 1 sheet of rub-on letters

☐ 2 brads

☐ 1 pen

☐ 3 photographs  **4×6**

To daddy they are work or landscape gloves. To you they are...

# eXPloRin
## gloves
You are so much more creative than daddy ☺

**Exploring Gloves** by Shannon Zickel
**Supplies** *Patterned papers:* Chatterbox and KI Memories; *Letter stickers:*
American Crafts and Heidi Swapp for Advantus; *Rub-on letters:* KI Memories;
*Brads:* American Crafts; *Pen:* Pigment Pro, American Crafts.

g

*exploring in the back yard—your favorite activity*

## INSTRUCTIONS

**1** Cut three strips of patterned paper. For a spontaneous look, vary the patterns and the length of the strips.

**2** Place three 4" x 6" pictures on the cardstock. Leave space for your title and journaling between two of the pictures.

**3** Apply letter stickers and rub-ons to create your title. Handwrite your journaling above and below the title.

## 30 minutes

- ☐ 2 sheets of cardstock
- ☐ 7 scraps of patterned paper (2 geometric, 1 floral, 3 striped, 1 text)
- ☐ 1 sheet of letter stickers
- ☐ 1 pen
- ☐ 4 brads
- ☐ 3 photographs **4×6**

## make it (even) easier!

Instead of creating your own flower accents from patterned-paper scraps, use premade flower embellishments.

### INSTRUCTIONS

1 Adhere photos to cardstock and add strips of patterned paper.

2 Create two petal templates (one large, one small) and cut seven petals for each using scraps of coordinating patterned papers. Arrange them into flower shapes and adhere them to your cardstock.

3 Using a pencil, draw a curved line from one flower to the other. Journal over the line and erase the pencil marks.

first Communion - November 19, 2005

**Anna's First Communion**
by Shannon Zickel
**Supplies** *Patterned papers:* Chatterbox, Scenic Route Paper Co., Making Memories, K&Company and Autumn Leaves; *Letter stickers:* Heidi Swapp for Advantus; *Brads and pen:* American Crafts.

## BONUS PROJECT

Don't let your scraps go to waste! Shannon created this darling card from the leftover scraps from her layout.

**Card (from "Anna's First Communion" scraps)** by Shannon Zickel
**Supplies** *Patterned papers:* Chatterbox, Scenic Route Paper Co., Making Memories, K&Company and Autumn Leaves; *Brads and pen:* American Crafts.

## 30 minutes

### from the pantry

- ☐ 3 sheets of cardstock
- ☐ 7 strips of patterned paper (2 floral, 2 geometric, 2 striped, 1 textured)
- ☐ 1 sheet of letter stickers
- ☐ 1 inkpad
- ☐ 1 computer font
- ☐ 4 photographs

## make it (even) easier!

Use a single large piece of patterned paper behind your photos and journaling strips.

## INSTRUCTIONS

1 Cut strips of patterned paper in various widths (from ¼" to ¾"). Ink the edges and attach the strips to your cardstock.

2 Trim three photos to fit on one page. Adhere the focal-point photo on the second page.

3 Cut your printed journaling into strips. Ink the edges and adhere them to your page. Apply letter stickers to create your title.

# Oo!

Playing hard. Dust in nose.

Three exhilarating sneezes.

One huge smile.

The simple pleasures...

This is the highlight of Xander's day.

**Ahh-Choo!** by April Peterson
**Supplies** *Textured cardstock:* Bazzill Basics Paper; *Patterned papers:* American Crafts, KI Memories and Anna Griffin; *Stickers:* Doodlebug Design; *Stamping ink:* ColorBox, Clearsnap; *Computer font:* 2Peas Weathered Fence, downloaded from *www.twopeasinabucket.com.*

## bonus project

Don't let your scraps go to waste! April created this darling card from the leftover scraps from her layout.

**Thank-You Card (from "Ahh-Choo!" scraps)** by April Peterson
**Supplies** *Textured cardstock:* Bazzill Basics Paper; *Patterned papers:* American Crafts, KI Memories and Anna Griffin; *Rub-on:* Karen Foster Design; *Stamping ink:* ColorBox, Clearsnap.

Thank you for your thoughtfulness

TOTAL TIME TO SCRAPLIFT:

## 45
minutes

### from the pantry

☐ 4 sheets of cardstock

☐ 8 strips of patterned paper
(4 striped, 4 textured)

☐ 2 computer fonts

☐ 4 photographs **4×6**

**Park Play** by Denine Zielinski
**Supplies** *Textured cardstock:* Prism Papers; *Patterned paper:* Carolee's
Creations; *Computer fonts:* Haettendchweiler, downloaded from the Internet;
2Peas Mister Giggles, downloaded from *www.twopeasinabucket.com.*

## make it
## (even) easier!

Create your title using letter
stickers or rub-ons instead
of cutting out the letters.

imb Up...Slide Down...Teeter Up...Totter Down...Spin Around...Swing Up High...Jump Around...Run and Play...

...er...wishing that the day would never end. There truly is no place that I'd rather be. --July 2004

## INSTRUCTIONS

1 Place your photos across the middle of the layout. Add strips of patterned paper above and below the photos.

2 Cut your printed journaling into strips and adhere them above and below the patterned paper.

3 Print your title backwards on a sheet of cardstock. Cut out the letters and adhere them to your page.

TOTAL TIME TO SCRAPLIFT:

## 20 minutes

### from the pantry

☐ 2 sheets of cardstock

☐ 4 strips of patterned paper (striped)

☐ 2 sheets of letter stickers

☐ 1 pen

☐ 5 photographs

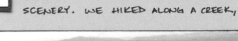

no Pai o gain

WORLD IT SURELY DID NOT DISAPPOINT
TERRIBLE BLISTER ON MY FOOT. I WAS
OF TIMES TO FIX MY BANDAGE   I
SCENERY. WE HIKED ALONG A CREEK,

**No Pain, No Gain** by Lisa Brown Caveney
**Supplies** *Patterned papers:* BasicGrey and unknown;
*Letter stickers:* BasicGrey; *Pen:* Zig Writer, EK Success.

WHEN DEREK AND I WERE IN NEW ZEALAND WE WANTED TO HIKE THE TONGORIRO CROSSING. TOUTED AS ONE OF THE BEST DAY HIKES IN THERE WAS ONLY ONE PROBLEM - JUST A SHORT WHILE INTO THE HIKE I GOT A DETERMINED HOWEVER. DESPITE THE PAIN AND NEEDING TO STOP A NUMBER MADE IT THROUGH THE HIKE. MY EFFORT WAS REWARDED WITH AMAZING INTO A CRATER, AND ALONG A RIDGELINE WITH BREATHTAKING VIEWS ALL THE WAY.

## INSTRUCTIONS

1 Attach a wide strip of cardstock across the middle of two sheets of patterned paper. Mat your focal-point photo and attach it to the top-left corner of the layout.

2 Crop four photos and attach them along the bottom of the layout. Using a marker, trace along the top and bottom of the photos to help draw attention to them.

3 Create the title with letter stickers (flipping the second half upside down), and handwrite your journaling on the cardstock strips.

TOTAL TIME TO SCRAPLIFT:

## 30
minutes

**from the pantry**

☐ 4 sheets of cardstock

☐ 1 sheet of patterned paper
(striped)

☐ 1 piece of ribbon

☐ 3 brads

☐ 1 computer font

☐ 1 inkpad

☐ 7 photographs

**Let's Go to the Carnival** by Leah LaMontagne
**Supplies** *Textured cardstock:* Prism Papers; *Patterned paper:* Making Memories;
*Ribbon:* Wrights; *Brads:* Queen & Co.; *Stamping ink:* ColorBox, Clearsnap;
*Computer font:* CK Corral, "Fresh Fonts" CD, *Creating Keepsakes.*

## make it
## (even) easier!

Skip inking the paper edges
if you're short on time.

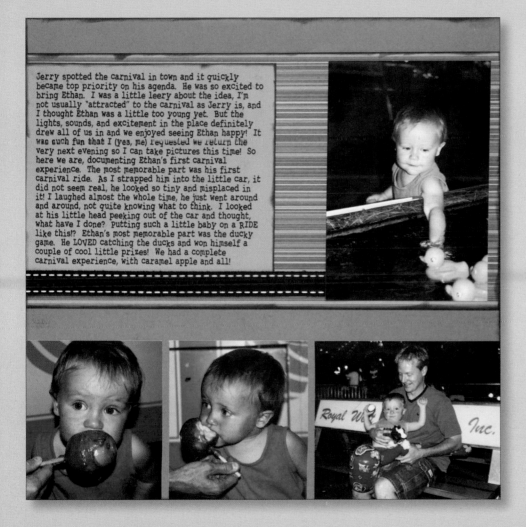

Jerry spotted the carnival in town and it quickly became top priority on his agenda. He was so excited to bring Ethan. I was a little leery about the idea, I'm not usually "attracted" to the carnival as Jerry is, and I thought Ethan was a little too young yet. But the lights, sounds, and excitement in the place definitely drew all of us in and we enjoyed seeing Ethan happy! It was such fun that I (yes, me) requested we return the very next evening so I can take pictures this time! So here we are, documenting Ethan's first carnival experience. The most memorable part was his first carnival ride. As I strapped him into the little car, it did not seem real, he looked so tiny and misplaced in it! I laughed almost the whole time, he just went around and around, not quite knowing what to think. I looked at his little head peeking out of the car and thought, what have I done? Putting such a little baby on a RIDE like this!? Ethan's most memorable part was the ducky game. He LOVED catching the ducks and won himself a couple of cool little prizes! We had a complete carnival experience, with caramel apple and all!

## INSTRUCTIONS

1 Cut the patterned paper in half. Ink the edges of the cardstock and patterned paper, then attach the patterned paper to the cardstock.

2 Ink the edges of the printed title and journaling blocks and attach them to your layout. Mat your focal-point photo and adhere all photos to the layout.

3 Embellish the page with a piece of ribbon and three brads.

TOTAL TIME TO SCRAPLIFT:

## 30
### minutes

### from the pantry

☐  2 sheets of cardstock

☐  1 strip of patterned paper
   (geometric)

☐  1 sheet of letter stickers

☐  1 computer font

☐  4 photographs

**Lake Erie** by Terri Davenport
**Supplies** *Textured cardstock:* Bazzill Basics Paper; *Patterned paper:* Center
City Designs; *Chipboard letters and punctuation:* Gin-X, Imagination Project;
*Computer font:* 2Peas Busy Babs, downloaded from *www.twopeasinabucket.com.*

## make it
## (even) easier!

Instead of printing
your journaling,
simply handwrite it.

## INSTRUCTIONS

1   Adhere photos to the cardstock at the bottom of the page. (*Tip:* It's quickest to work from left to right.) Instead of measuring and cutting the bottom horizontal photo, simply tuck it under the top photo.

2   Adhere a strip of patterned paper on the bottom-right side of the layout. You don't need to measure the width—just tuck any excess under the photos.

3   Create your title using letter stickers. Print your journaling on a scrap of cardstock and attach it over the patterned paper.

TOTAL TIME TO SCRAPLIFT:

# 30
## minutes

## from the pantry

☐ 1 sheet of cardstock

☐ 2 sheets of patterned paper
(geometric)

☐ 1 sheet of rub-on letters

☐ 1 pen

☐ 3 photographs

JULY 27, 2005

**GROSS**

GROSSOLOGY EXHIBIT. SCIENCE MUSEUM.

YEP. THAT'S POOP YOU'RE LOOKING AT! AND WHY, MAY YOU ASK, DID I BRING YOU TO STUDY POOP? WELL FIRST, BECAUSE YOU ASKED ME TO! AND SECOND, I THINK ANY PLACE THAT SPONSORS AN EXHIBIT LIKE THIS IS DOWNRIGHT COOL WHAT BETTER WAY TO GET YOU EXCITED ABOUT LEARNING THAN FINDING STUFF THAT IS INTERESTING TO YOU KIDS, EVEN IF IT IS A BIT ON THE UM, SHALL WE SAY, DISGUSTING SIDE!

You may think that if you've seen one poop, you've seen them all. The fact is, different animals make different caca. Texture and shape are important for feces identification. Here are some of the common names and characteristics of animal fec

Scat – wild animals, mountain lions, coyotes, wolves. If you're familiar with do and cat poo, wild dog and cat caca look similar to your pets' poo. However, coyotes and cougars don't get canned kibble so their poo may contain fur and bones. Hairs in the feces hold the poop mass together. If you see scratch marks on the ground in an attempt to cover the dump, it is probably a wild cat.

Pellets, Droppings, Road Apples – deer, elk,

droppings tells you a rabbit, deer, m

be of ga

**Gross** by Rhonda Stark
**Supplies** *Software:* Adobe Photoshop, Adobe Systems; *Digital patterned papers:* Gina Cabrera, *www.digitaldesignessentials.com; Computer fonts:* TIA A Capital Idea by Tia Bennett, *www. designerdigitals.com;* Shortcut, downloaded from *www.dafont.com.*

## INSTRUCTIONS

1 Crop your patterned paper and photos and place them on your layout.

2 Add a rub-on title.

3 Handwrite your journaling.

## 30 minutes

october 2005

almost there .. almost there .. almost there .. almost there

**success is sweet**

especially when you work hard for it you used to be afraid to walk this all by yourself, but with hard work and determination you mastered it try to remember that lesson erin!

**Success Is Sweet** by Rhonda Stark
**Supplies** *Software:* Adobe Photoshop, Adobe Systems; *Digital kraft and patterned papers:* Gina Cabrera, *www.digitaldesignessentials.com; Digital journaling stamp:* Katie Pertiet, *www.designerdigitals.com; Computer fonts:* TIA Moxie by Tia Bennett, *www.designerdigitals.com;* Broken 15, downloaded from the Internet.

## from the pantry

☐ 1 sheet of cardstock

☐ 2 strips of patterned paper (floral)

☐ 1 set of letter stamps

☐ 1 lined stamp

☐ 2 inkpads

☐ 1 pen

☐ 3 photographs

## INSTRUCTIONS

1 Crop the patterned paper and photos and place them on a piece of cardstock.

2 Stamp the lines for your accents and journaling. Stamp the title.

3 Handwrite your journaling.

TOTAL TIME TO SCRAPLIFT:

## 30 minutes

## from the pantry

- ☐ 3 sheets of patterned paper (1 striped, 1 geometric, 1 textured)

- ☐ 1 sheet of letter stickers

- ☐ 2 pens

- ☐ 4 photographs

**Swim of a Lifetime** by Rhonda Stark
**Supplies** *Software:* Adobe Photoshop, Adobe Systems; *Digital patterned papers:* Katie Pertiet, *www. designerdigitals.com; Digital chipboard letters (re-colored):* Chunky Chipboard Alphas by Katie Pertiet, *www.designerdigitals.com; Computer fonts:* Susie's Hand, downloaded from the Internet; TIA A Capital Idea by Tia Bennett, *www.designerdigitals.com.*

## INSTRUCTIONS

1   Crop the patterned paper and photos and arrange them on your patterned-paper background.

2   Apply letter stickers to create the first word of your title. Write the rest of the title underneath the stickers.

3   Handwrite your journaling.

## a just for me WEEKEND

This was my second mother/daughter weekend away, and it was just as enjoyable as the first. We all met in Brown County Indiana for a weekend of shopping. I wasn't sure if I'd enjoy the shopping part, but the town was just so quaint and had lots of great garden shops and even a few clothes boutiques. I was even able to pick up a really cool coat. I had brought my new camera along to play and had fun going out and just taking some photos of the things that interested me. I was thrilled with some of the shots I got. But the most enjoyable part had to be the company. It was good to see everyone again and reconnect. I have enjoyed getting to know Jim's side of the family a little better. And I look forward to our next trip in 2006.

**A Weekend Just for Me** by Rhonda Stark
**Supplies** *Software:* Adobe Photoshop, Adobe Systems; *Digital patterned papers and digital date stamp:* Katie Pertiet, *www.designerdigitals.com; Computer fonts:* Artistamp Medium and Susie's Hand, downloaded from the Internet.

### from the pantry

- ☐ 1 sheet of cardstock
- ☐ 1 sheets of patterned paper (floral)
- ☐ 2 sheets of rub-on letters
- ☐ 1 rub-on seal
- ☐ 1 pen
- ☐ 3 photographs

## INSTRUCTIONS

1 Crop the patterned paper and photos and arrange them on your layout.

2 Apply rub-on letters to create your title.

3 Handwrite your journaling.

TOTAL TIME TO SCRAPLIFT:

## 30
minutes

### from the pantry

☐ 2 sheets of cardstock

☐ 8 strips of patterned paper
(2 striped, 2 geometric,
1 textured, 3 text)

☐ 1 sheet of letter stickers

☐ 2 accent or dingbat stickers
from the letter sticker sheet

☐ 2 brads

☐ 1 paper clip

☐ 1 pen

☐ 4 photographs

**New Target** by Shannon Zickel
**Supplies** *Patterned papers and letter stickers:* Making Memories; *Brads:* Lost
Art Treasures; *Pen:* Pigment Pro, American Crafts; *Paper clip:* 7gypsies.

## INSTRUCTIONS

1    Layer patterned paper over the cardstock background. Trim four 4" x 6" photos to 3" x 6" and line them up along the bottom of the page.

2    Use letter stickers to create your title.

3    Attach small journaling strips written on patterned paper to your page with mini brads and a paper clip.

## 30
minutes

## from the pantry

- ☐ 5 sheets of cardstock
- ☐ 1 piece of patterned paper (striped)
- ☐ 1 sheet of letter stickers
- ☐ 1 pen
- ☐ 5 photographs **4×6**

first christmas in our hor

Christmas this year was very special for us because we got to
both our families at our home for the first time. We only got
house a few weeks before the holidays so it was a lot of
to get everything done in time but we did it. It was
mixing both family's Scandanavian, Polish, and English tra-
for our celebration. The very best part was having the whole
together for the holidays. I hope this is the first of

**First Christmas in Our Home** by Lisa Brown Caveney
**Supplies** *Cardstock and patterned paper:* KI Memories; *Letter stickers:*
Chatterbox; *Pen:* Gelly Roll, Sakura.

## INSTRUCTIONS

1 Create the background using a strip of cardstock on the bottom, a strip of cardstock in another color in the middle and striped patterned paper at the top. (*Tip:* Miter the edges of the patterned paper for a framed look.)

2 Mat four 4" x 6" photos together and attach them to your layout. Mat your focal-point photo separately and attach it to the bottom-right corner of the right page.

3 Create your title with letter stickers, and handwrite your journaling.

## 30 minutes

### from the pantry

- ☐ 3 sheets of cardstock
- ☐ 2 sheets of letter stickers
- ☐ 2 punctuation accents from letter sticker sheet
- ☐ 6 pieces of ribbon
- ☐ 1 pen
- ☐ 1 brad
- ☐ 6 staples
- ☐ 5 photographs

**Turning Seven** by Shannon Zickel
**Supplies** *Letter stickers, ribbon, brads and pen:* American Crafts; *Other:* Staples.

{ seven friends over to spend the night. racing to dress up like pirates - sword fights - all before settling in for Pirates of the Caribbean outside on a 12 foot screen drive in style - what a great party! }

## INSTRUCTIONS

1 Trim five 4" x 6" photos to 3¼" x 5¼" and line them up along the center of the layout. Leave a slight space between each one.

2 Apply letter stickers to the top of the page to create the first word of the title. Add letter stickers over the photos to spell out the second word.

3 Use staples to attach small scraps of ribbon. Apply two punctuation or dingbat stickers from your sheet of letter stickers, and handwrite your journaling between them.

TOTAL TIME TO SCRAPLIFT:

# 30
## minutes

## from the pantry

- ☐ 2 sheets of cardstock

- ☐ 6 strips of patterned paper
  (5 striped, 1 text)

- ☐ 3–6 sheets of letter stickers
  (*Tip:* Use leftovers from
  multiple sheets.)

- ☐ 1 sheet of rub-on letters

- ☐ 2 brads

- ☐ 1 pen

- ☐ 1 small circle punch

- ☐ 5 photographs

## make it
## (even) easier!

Instead of mixing
and matching stickers,
use just one set.

**Christmas Morning Excitement** by Shannon Zickel
**Supplies** *Patterned papers:* Scenic Route Paper Co. and KI Memories; *Letter stickers:* Scrapworks (fabric), Doodlebug Design (black) and American Crafts (all others); *Rub-on letters and circle stickers:* KI Memories; *Brads:* American Crafts; *Pen:* Pigment Pro, American Crafts.

So excited to open all your presents... the expressions on your face bring us so much joy!

chRiStmas
-morning-
excitement
-December 25, 2005-

## INSTRUCTIONS

1 Attach five strips of patterned paper in a random pattern on the left page. Attach one strip on the left edge of the right page. Vary the height and width of the papers for a fun look. Use a circle or hole punch to create three circular accents from your patterned-paper scraps.

2 Trim five 4"x 6" photos to 3¼" x 5¼" and line them up in the middle of the layout. Leave a slight space between each photo.

3 Create your title from various letter stickers in the bottom right portion of your layout. Write your journaling above the photos on the right page. (*Tip:* Back a couple of sticker matrixes with patterned paper and use them as letter stickers, too!)

TOTAL TIME TO SCRAPLIFT:

# 30
minutes

## from the pantry

☐ 3 sheets of cardstock

☐ 3 sheets of patterned paper
(2 geometric, 1 textured)

☐ 1 sheet of letter stickers

☐ 1 piece of ribbon

☐ 1 pen

☐ 5 photographs

**Sister Vacation** by Lisa Brown Caveney
**Supplies** *Patterned papers:* BasicGrey and source unknown; *Letter stickers:*
Creative Imaginations; *Ribbon:* May Arts; *Pen:* Zig Writer, EK Success.

WHEN MISSY SUGGESTED THAT WE TAKE A VACATION TOGETHER BEFORE I STARTED MY NEW JOB I JUMPED AT THE CHANCE. SHE FOUND US A GREAT DEAL THROUGH APPLE VACATIONS STAYING AT SUNSCAPE TULUM. IT WAS AWESOME. THERE WEREN'T ANY OTHER RESORTS NEARBY SO WE WALKED ON THE BEACH FOR HOURS WITHOUT RUNNING INTO ANYONE. WE ALSO WENT SIGHTSEEING VISITING THE AMAZING MAYAN RUINS AT CHICHEN ITZA AND TULUM. WE ALSO SPENT A DAY SNORKELING AND A DAY TOURING AND SHOPPING IN PLAYA DEL CARMEN. WE HAD A GREAT RELAXING AND SPENDING TIME TOGETHER. I'M GLAD WE TOOK A SISTER VACATION. 10/05

Sister Vacation

## INSTRUCTIONS

1 Group different patterned papers together to create your background.

2 Crop four 4" x 6" photos to 4" x 5½" and attach them to the left side of the layout. Mat your focal point photo and attach it to the bottom-right corner of the right page.

3 Apply letter stickers to create your title. Embellish the layout with a simple ribbon border along the left edge of the photos. Handwrite your journaling.

# 30
## minutes

## from the pantry

- ☐ 5 sheets of cardstock

- ☐ 2 strips of patterned paper (geometric)

- ☐ 1 set of letter stamps

- ☐ 1 inkpad

- ☐ 1 pen

- ☐ 8 pieces of rickrack

- ☐ 2 circle punches (1 large, 1 small)

- ☐ 4 photographs

**This Smile … This Girl** by Michaela Young-Mitchell
**Supplies** *Textured cardstock:* Bazzill Basics Paper; *Patterned paper and letter stamps:* Karen Foster Design; *Stamping ink:* Close To My Heart; *Circle punches:* CARL Mfg.; *Rickrack:* Wrights; *Pen:* Zig Writer, EK Success.

## make it (even) easier!

Use ribbon or strips of patterned paper instead of rickrack.

Instead of stamping the title, use letter stickers or rub-ons.

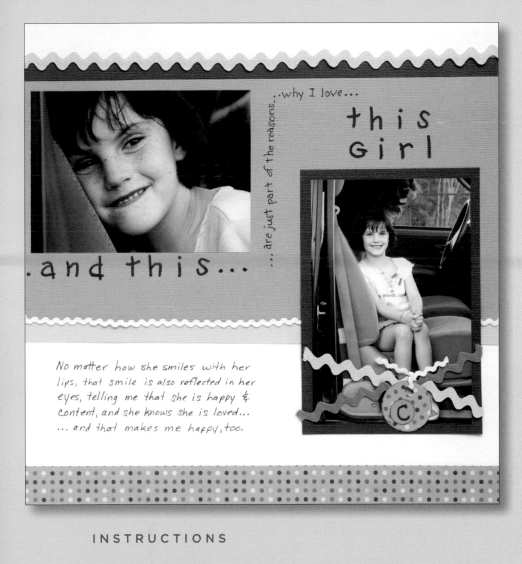

...why I love...

...are just part of the reasons...

this Girl

..and this...

No matter how she smiles with her lips, that smile is also reflected in her eyes, telling me that she is happy & content, and she knows she is loved... ... and that makes me happy, too.

## INSTRUCTIONS

1 Trim strips of cardstock and patterned paper and layer them on the background.

2 Embellish the cardstock borders with rickrack. Arrange your photos and adhere them to the layout. Punch a small circle and large circle out of patterned paper to create a tag.

3 Stamp key words of the title and fill in the rest with your handwriting. Handwrite your journaling.

TOTAL TIME TO SCRAPLIFT:

## 45
minutes

**Disney World** by Shannon Taylor
**Supplies** *Letter stickers:* Mustard Moon; *Ribbon:* C.M. Offray & Son; *Brads:* American Crafts; *Pen:* Zig Writer, EK Success.

## make it
## (even) easier!

Use strips of
patterned paper instead
of the ribbon.

## INSTRUCTIONS

1 Group your photos together, trimming them to create one large block of photos. Attach them to your layout. Handwrite your journaling, mat it and attach it to your layout.

2 Apply letter stickers to create your title. Pair a black cardstock circle with three black brads to make a "Mickey ears" accent.

3 Embellish the page with strips of ribbon and a row of brads.

# 10 easy techniques

Create cool accents and embellishments using just the basics. Give these 10 great ideas a try:

1  Cut petals from various patterned papers. Adhere them to your cardstock and place a brad in the center. Let your handwritten journaling serve as a flower stem or vine.
—*Shannon Zickel, Page 70*

2  Create a cool effect reminiscent of a mirror image by placing half of your title letter stickers upside down underneath the first half. If your title is short, you could even repeat your title upside down underneath the original title.
—*Lisa Brown Caveney, Page 76*

3 Emphasize one or two letter stickers in a title by cutting out the sticker matrix and backing it with colorful patterned paper.
—*Shannon Zickel, Page 92*

4  Create a special border using a strip of patterned paper, pieces of ribbon and brads. Use the brads to attach the ribbon to the paper. Use the paper's pattern to determine spacing. Notice how the brads continue the dotted pattern of the paper.
—*Denine Zielinski, Page 101*

5  Cut flowers, circles or other accents from patterned paper. For additional emphasis, adhere them to your page using adhesive dots or colored brads.
—*Kim Kesti, Page 109*

6 Overlap your title with your journaling text. Here, I used a computer font for the title and a pen to write my journaling. You can get the same look using letter stamps or rub-ons for your title and a pen for your journaling.
—*Lisa Brown Caveney, Page 116*

7 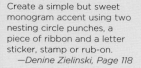 Create a simple but sweet monogram accent using two nesting circle punches, a piece of ribbon and a letter sticker, stamp or rub-on.
—*Denine Zielinski, Page 118*

8 Tie a piece of ribbon or rickrack to a paper clip to create a cute and easy accent. Clip it to a photo for a whimsical look.
—*Wendy Sue Anderson, Page 142*

9  Let your journaling do double duty as a stylish border. Journal on a piece of cardstock, then cut out each individual word. Adhere the words around your photos or the edges of the page.
—*Mimi Schramm, Page 144*

10  Give your child a piece of cardstock to draw on. Cut up his or her artwork to use as accents on your pages.
—*Moon Ko, Page 145*

1
hour

**Our Special Tree** by Denine Zielinski
**Supplies** *Patterned Papers:* Imagination Project and Daisy D's Paper Co.; *Rub-on letters:* KI Memories; *Ribbon:* American Crafts; *Brads:* Making Memories; *Computer Font:* Bernhart, Bay Animatons, Inc.

## from the pantry

☐ 2 sheets of cardstock

☐ 4 strips of patterned paper (2 geometric, 2 textured)

☐ 1 computer font

☐ 1 sheet of rub-on letters

☐ 13 brads

☐ 10 pieces of ribbon

☐ 4 photographs 4×6

## INSTRUCTIONS

1  Arrange your photos on the cardstock. Print your journaling on patterned paper and attach it next to the photos. Add torn strips of patterned paper to the left and right edges of the layout.

2  Apply rub-on letters to create the title. Attach journaling strips with mini brads.

3  Fold ribbons along the left edge of your page and attach them with mini brads.

## make it (even) easier!

Attach the ribbon strips to the page with staples instead of mini brads.

## 45 minutes

- ☐ 2 sheets of cardstock

- ☐ 3 strips of patterned paper (striped)

- ☐ 19 brads

- ☐ 4 sheets of letter stickers (*Tip:* Mix and match your leftovers.)

- ☐ 1 pen

- ☐ 3 photographs

**This Is Not a Good Idea** by Shannon Zickel
**Supplies** *Patterned paper, letter stickers, brads and pen:* American Crafts.

## make it (even) easier!

Stamp a design around the focal point of your photo instead of circling it with brads. Use a solvent-based ink, such as Tsukineko's StazOn, when stamping directly on photographs.

ot a good idea

Jake's homemade haircut - Aug'05

## INSTRUCTIONS

1   Adhere the first two photos to your layout. Trim the third photo so it's slightly shorter than the first two.

2   Attach brads in a circle around the subject of your first photo. To do this, create a circle template, then use a paper piercer to create evenly spaced holes.

3   Apply letter stickers to create your title. For additional visual interest, place part of your title vertically and the other part horizontally. Finish the layout with a few strips of patterned paper.

# 30 minutes

## from the pantry

- ☐ 5 sheets of cardstock
- ☐ 1 sheet of patterned paper (geometric)
- ☐ 1 piece of ribbon
- ☐ 1 computer font
- ☐ 3 circle punches (various sizes)
- ☐ 4 photographs 4×6

**Cranberry Harvest** by Sue Thomas
**Supplies** *Textured cardstock:* Prism Papers; *Patterned paper:* Scenic Route Paper Co.; *Circle punch:* EK Success; *Ribbon:* May Arts; *Computer font:* AL Constitution, "15 Vintage Fonts" CD, Autumn Leaves.

## make it (even) easier!

If you're not comfortable printing your title, use letter stickers, rub-ons or stamps.

## INSTRUCTIONS

1 Print your title vertically on a sheet of cardstock.

2 Group your photos together and mat them. Attach them to your cardstock. Cut long strips of patterned paper and place them around the matted photos.

3 Punch small cardstock circles and adhere them to your layout. Tie a ribbon in a bow and affix it to the page.

TOTAL TIME TO SCRAPLIFT:

## 30
minutes

### from the pantry

- ☐ 2 sheets of cardstock

- ☐ 3 strips of patterned paper
  (1 striped, 1 floral, 1 geometric)

- ☐ 3–5 sheets of letter stickers
  (*Tip:* Mix and match various
  leftovers.)

- ☐ 2 brads

- ☐ 1 pen

- ☐ 5 photographs

**Leaf Fight with a Friend** by Shannon Zickel
**Supplies** *Patterned papers:* Scenic Route Paper Co. and My Mind's Eye; *Letter stickers:* Scrapworks, Heidi Swapp for Advantus and American Crafts; *Brads:* American Crafts; *Pen:* Pigment Pro, American Crafts.

Shelby and Jake enjoying the over abundance of fallen leaves – and each other – as usual!
— October 2005 —

## INSTRUCTIONS

1  Attach your focal-point photo to the top-right section of your layout. Trim the others to line up along the bottom of the layout.

2  Cut three strips of patterned paper and attach them, overlapping, on the left side of the left-hand page.

3  Fill in the center area between the patterned paper and focal-point photo with a letter-sticker title and handwritten journaling.

TOTAL TIME TO SCRAPLIFT:

## 30 minutes

### from the pantry

☐ 1 sheet of cardstock

☐ 1 set of letter stamps

☐ 1 rub-on letter

☐ 1 computer font

☐ 1 letter sticker

☐ 1 inkpad

☐ 1 circle punch

☐ 2 photographs

## make it (even) easier!

Print your journaling on a separate piece of cardstock and cut it to fit.

**SWIMMING BRAVERY!**

**progress**

Swimming lessons in a nutshell? What started out as a full-fledged nightmare, has gradually become a good experience. But we were sure worried at first. Worried that we had pushed you too hard, at too young of an age to do something you weren't quite ready for. The first several lessons had you in near hysterics, particularly when you had to put your face into the water. You screamed blue-bloody murder for most of these lessons. It was a bit better the times that Daddy went in with you, but it wasn't until Lesson #5 that the tide suddenly turned. I went in with you, and surprisingly, you didn't cry (well until you were asked to don a life-jacket...by this point you already figured you could swim well enough to not need one. A good dose of your Father's ego here to be sure). All the talking and out-of-pool lessons we had done during the week seemed to have helped boost your confidence. Lesson #6 you went in by yourself and did so incredibly well. With two lessons left, I don't think you'll pass, and that's OK. I'm just so proud of you for overcoming your fears and being so brave! On Sunday, we went to Opa and Oma's and you went for a nice swim with Daddy. Kicking on the kickboard, jumping in from the edge, and in general, having a wonderful time. Before I know it, you're going to be swimming on your own. **yay!**

**Swimming Bravery** by Rachel Ludwig
**Supplies** *Textured cardstock:* Bazzill Basics Paper; *Letter stamps:* Educational Insights; *Stamping ink:* Nick Bantock, Ranger Industries; *Rub-on:* Autumn Leaves; *"E" letter sticker:* Li'l Davis Designs; *Computer font:* Arial, Microsoft Word.

### INSTRUCTIONS

1 Print your journaling directly on a sheet of cardstock. (*Tip:* Adjust the left margin in your word-processing program so the text begins in the middle of the page.)

2 Line up the photos vertically and punch a half circle on the right edge where they line up. Place a letter sticker in the punched-out space.

3 Stamp your title and embellish the page with a rub-on letter.

## 20 minutes

### from the pantry

☐ 2 sheets of cardstock

☐ 1 sheet of patterned paper (floral)

☐ 1 sheet of rub-on letters

☐ 3 brads

☐ 1 pen

☐ 1 corner rounder

☐ 3 photographs **4×6**

silly
birthday
treats

Sophie, lydia, haley, mia ... 2006

**Silly Birthday Treats** by Kim Kesti
**Supplies** *Textured cardstock and large brads:* Bazzill Basics Paper; *Patterned paper:* Gin-X, Imagination Project; *Rub-ons:* Scrapworks; *Corner rounder:* Creative Memories.

## make it (even) easier!

Instead of cutting out flower images from patterned paper, use flower stickers.

**Supplies** *Textured cardstock:* Hot Off The Press; *Flower stickers:* Sandylion; *Brads:* American Crafts.

## INSTRUCTIONS

1 Round the corners of your photos and photo mat. Adhere the photos to the mat, then adhere the mat to the background cardstock.

2 Cut out flowers from patterned paper and adhere them to the page. Randomly attach brads as page accents.

3 Apply rub-ons to create the title, and handwrite your journaling.

TOTAL TIME TO SCRAPLIFT:

# 1 hour

## from the pantry

☐ 3 sheets of cardstock

☐ 2 sheets of patterned paper (1 striped, 1 geometric)

☐ 1 rub-on letter

☐ 1 computer font

☐ 2 circle punches (1 large, 1 small)

☐ 9 photographs

Birthday number four... My goodness! I can't believe it. You are four years old. FOUR! We celebrated your birthday with family this year as we always do. Grandma and Grandpa Gailey, and Auntie and Bradford were all in attendance. You also had a small party at pre-kindergarten. We brought a cake in for you to share with your classmates and you really dug that. We haven't gone down the path of the kid party yet... maybe next year. Your Grandma and Grandpa got you a shake racing car set, which of course Grandma played with you. You shake the cars and they go. No batteries needed. Very cool! They also got you a real piggy bank. Grandpa even gave you $6.00 plus a bunch of change to put in it. Momma and Daddy got you a Read with Me DVD thingamabob plus a Candy Land board game. Your Auntie and Uncle Bradford got you a soccer ball, a skateboard and pads. You have it good little man! I had your cake ordered special from a local bakery and it was yummy, although next time I won't get the chocolate mousse for the filling. It was a tad bit bitter. Oh well, better luck next year. You certainly didn't seem to mind though and of course you really enjoyed the ice cream. You wouldn't be a Gailey if you didn't! 11/4/05

**4** by Ashley Gailey
**Supplies** *Textured cardstock:* Bazzill Basics Paper; *Patterned papers:* Chatterbox; *Circle punches:* EK Success and McGill; *Rub-ons:* Making Memories; *Computer font:* Euromode, downloaded from the Internet.

## INSTRUCTIONS

**1** Trim six photos to 4" x 5" and line them up across both pages of the layout. Line up three photos underneath them, leaving a space for your journaling.

**2** Attach strips of cardstock and patterned paper to the top of the layout. Separate the two rows of photos with a strip of patterned paper.

**3** Attach the journaling block. Embellish the page with a monogram circle punched from two scraps of cardstock.

## TOTAL TIME TO SCRAPLIFT:

# 25
## minutes

## from the pantry

- ☐ 2 sheets of cardstock
- ☐ 1 piece of patterned paper (floral)
- ☐ 2 pieces of ribbon
- ☐ 12 brads
- ☐ 2 sheets of rub-on letters
- ☐ 1 pen
- ☐ 3 photographs

## make it (even) easier!

Omit the ribbons
and brads for a
super-fast page.

## INSTRUCTIONS >

1 Arrange the patterned paper and green cardstock strips on a sheet of white cardstock.

2 Attach the photos to the page. Place a piece of ribbon underneath the photos. Tie a piece of ribbon into a bow and affix it to the center of the first ribbon.

3 Apply the rub-ons to create the title and photo captions. Handwrite your journaling, and accent the page with brads.

## bonus project

Don't let your project scraps go to waste! Leah created this darling card from the leftover scraps from her layout.

**On Your Wedding Card (from "The Happy Couple" scraps)** by Leah LaMontagne
**Supplies** *Textured cardstock:* Prism Papers; *Patterned paper:* Magic Scraps; *Ribbon:* Making Memories; *Rub-ons:* Making Memories (large) and Heidi Swapp for Advantus (small); *Pen:* Pigma Micron, Sakura.

The Happy

# COUPLE

GROOM

BRIDE

I was able to spend a little extra time with the couple while photographing them. It was such a special treat to see how happy they were this day. Totally in love, completely enjoying their beautiful celebration. Congratulations Joel and Michelle!

April 17, 2004

**The Happy Couple** by Leah LaMontagne
**Supplies** *Textured cardstock:* Prism Papers; *Patterned paper:* Magic Scraps; *Ribbon:* Making Memories; *Brads:* Queen & Co.;
*Rub-ons:* Making Memories (large) and Heidi Swapp for Advantus (small); *Pen:* Pigma Micron, Sakura.

TOTAL TIME TO SCRAPLIFT:

# 30
## minutes

## from the pantry

☐ 2 sheets of cardstock

☐ 2 sheets of patterned paper
(1 floral, 1 striped)

☐ 12 brads

☐ 1 sheet of letter stickers

☐ 1 pen

☐ 4 photographs

## INSTRUCTIONS >

1 Center a large rectangle of cardstock on the background page. Add patterned-paper triangles to two corners.

2 Arrange your photos, then add the title and brad embellishments.

3 Add a strip of patterned paper near bottom of the page and handwrite your journaling.

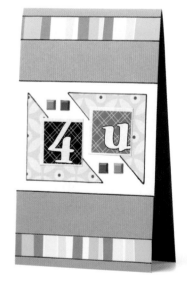

# bonus project

Don't let your project scraps go to waste! Leah created this darling card from the leftover scraps from her layout.

**4 U Card (from "Beach" scraps)** by Leah LaMontagne
**Supplies** *Patterned paper:* Cross-My-Heart; *Letter stickers:* Scenic Route Paper Co.; *Brads:* Magic Scraps; *Pen:* Zig Writer, EK Success.

# beach

A day at the beach is few and far between for us... so we greatly appreciate what we can get! Today was incredible fun! Ethan lost himself in the sand...playing all day, non-stop! The waves were so awesome, big enough to toss you in an adventure, yet still manageable. It was fabulous. Everyone found themselves enjoying every minute.

Sunday, Sept. 5th, 2004. Leah, Jerry, Ethan, Mom, Dad, Janelle, Jessica, Anna, Gabrielle, Josh and Candice... all loving the California Coast. Till next time!!!

**Beach** by Leah LaMontagne
**Supplies** *Patterned papers:* Cross-My-Heart; *Letter stickers:* Scenic Route Paper Co.; *Brads:* Magic Scraps; *Pen:* Zig Writer, EK Success.

TOTAL TIME TO SCRAPLIFT:

# 20
minutes

## from the pantry

- ☐ 3 sheets of cardstock
- ☐ 1 computer font
- ☐ 1 pen
- ☐ 10 photographs

WHEN DEREK AND I WANT TO GET A PHOTO TOGETHER, WE DON'T LET THE LACK OF SOMEONE ELSE TO SNAP THE SHOT STOP US. WE HOLD THE CAMERA OUT IN FRONT OF US AND TAKE THE PICTURE OURSELVES. L to R, T to B — ONE YEAR ANNIVERSARY, UPGRADED TO FIRST CLASS ON OUR HONEYMOON, ON A BOAT OFF GRAND CAYMAN, HIKING IN THE SIERRA MOUNTAINS, STANDING AT CAPE POINT IN SOUTH AFRICA, RIVERBOAT RIDE IN BELIZE, OUR COTTAGE IN THE DRAKENSBERG MOUNTAINS, HEADING OFF FOR A NIGHT AT THE BALLET, TAKING A JUNGLE CANOPY TOUR IN HONDURAS, WALKING IN THE EVERGLADES. THEY MAY NOT BE THE GREATEST PHOTOS BUT I'M GLAD WE TOOK THESE SELF - PORTRAITS.

**SELF PORTRAIT**

**Self Portrait** by Lisa Brown Caveney
**Supplies** *Pen:* Zig Writer, EK Success; *Computer font:* AL Highlight, "15 Essential Fonts" CD, Autumn Leaves.

## INSTRUCTIONS

1 Crop nine photos into 3½" squares and arrange them in a grid on the right side of the layout.

2 Print out your title, attach it to the top-left corner of the layout and then journal over it.

3 Attach a horizontal 4" x 6" photo to the bottom-left corner of the layout.

## 30 minutes

- ☐ 3 sheets of cardstock

- ☐ 2 strips of patterned paper (striped)

- ☐ 1 sheet of letter stickers

- ☐ 1 sheet of rub-on letters

- ☐ 2 circle punches (1 large, 1 small)

- ☐ 1 corner rounder punch

- ☐ 1 computer font

- ☐ 1 piece of ribbon

- ☐ 3 photographs

**Birthday Bash** by Denine Zielinski
**Supplies** *Textured cardstock:* Bazzill Basics Paper; *Patterned paper, rub-ons and letter stickers:* Arctic Frog; *Ribbon:* May Arts; *Corner rounder:* EK Success; *Circle punches:* Marvy Uchida; *Computer font:* Century Gothic, Microsoft Word.

## INSTRUCTIONS

1 Create a title block using rub-ons and letter stickers on a 9" x 2¾" piece of cardstock.

2 Line up your photos on the page and place the title block beneath the photos. Place your printed journaling beneath the title block.

3 Use a corner rounder to round two corners on each strip of patterned paper. Place the strips on each side of the photo, title and journaling blocks. Add a circle monogram accent to the top of your photos.

**costume change**

SCHOOL PARTY    Trunk or TREAT    TRICK or TREAT

WHEN You're thE younGest, You can Have A diffErent costume for everY event.

**Costume Change** by Terri Davenport
**Supplies** *Textured cardstock:* Prism Papers; *Patterned papers and rub-ons:* Gin-X, Imagination Project; *Letter stickers:* Chatterbox.

TOTAL TIME TO SCRAPLIFT:

## 20 minutes

### from the pantry

- ☐ 2 sheets of cardstock

- ☐ 3 strips of patterned paper (1 striped, 2 geometric)

- ☐ 1 sheet of letter stickers

- ☐ 1 sheet of rub-on letters

- ☐ 3 photographs

## INSTRUCTIONS

1 Line up three rectangles of patterned paper along the center of the page. Adhere a photo to each rectangle.

2 Cut tabs from cardstock and round the corners. Adhere one over each photo.

3 Apply stickers and rub-ons to create your title, photo captions and journaling.

## make it (even) easier!

Instead of using three different patterned paper designs, choose just one.

TOTAL TIME TO SCRAPLIFT:

## 45
minutes

- ☐ 2 sheets of cardstock

- ☐ 2 strips of patterned paper (striped)

- ☐ 3 sheets of letter stickers

- ☐ 1 sheet of rub-on numbers

- ☐ 1 circle punch

- ☐ 1 pen

- ☐ 9 photographs

**Summer Sunday Nights** by Shannon Zickel
**Supplies** *Patterned paper:* American Crafts; *Letter stickers:* American Crafts, Making Memories and Doodlebug Design; *Round rub-on numbers:* Making Memories; *Pen:* Pigment Pro, American Crafts; *Other:* Circle punch.

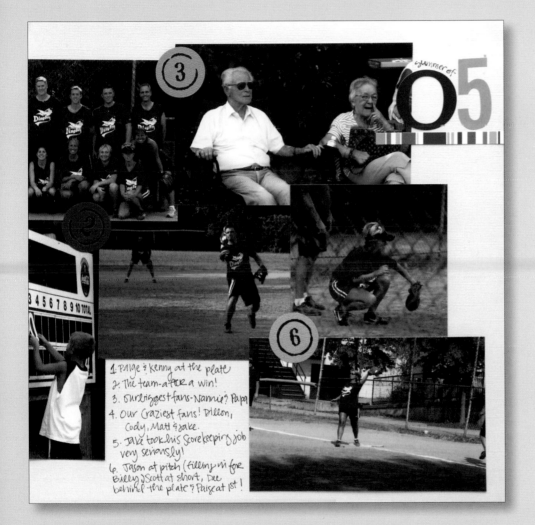

Handwritten journaling on layout:

1. Paige & Kenny at the plate
2. The team—after a win!
3. Our biggest fans—Nannie & Papa
4. Our craziest fans! Dillon, Cody, Matt & Jake.
5. Jake took his scorekeeping job very seriously!
6. Jason at pitch (filling in for Billy) Scott at short, Dee behind the plate & Paige at 1st!

## INSTRUCTIONS

1 Arrange three vertical photos and six horizontal photos (all 4" x 6") on the layout.

2 Attach a strip of patterned paper across the center of the left page. Layer random letter stickers over the strip to create the title.

3 Punch cardstock circles and apply rub-on numbers to label the photos. Handwrite your journaling and photo captions.

TOTAL TIME TO SCRAPLIFT:

## 20 minutes

### from the pantry

☐ 3 sheets of cardstock

☐ 1 sheet of patterned paper (text)

☐ 2 pieces of rickrack

☐ 8 staples

☐ 1 sheet of letter stickers

☐ 1 sheet of rub-on letters

☐ 1 pen

☐ 1 inkpad

☐ 5 photographs

## make it (even) easier!

Skip the inked edges to make this layout easier.

**My Sweethearts** by Wendy Sue Anderson
**Supplies** *Patterned paper, rickrack and rub-on letters:* Doodlebug Design; *Staples:* Making Memories; *Letter stickers:* American Crafts; *Pen:* Zig Writer, EK Success; *Stamping ink:* Memories, Stewart Superior Corporation.

## INSTRUCTIONS

1 Mount your focal-point photo on patterned paper. Rub the edges with black ink, then mat again on black cardstock. Adhere the matted photo to the left page of the layout. On the right page, attach four photos in a grid pattern.

2 Ink the edges of a strip of patterned paper and attach it to the top of the right page. Add stickers to create the title, apply a rub-on date, and handwrite your journaling.

3 Finish the design by stapling two pieces of rickrack to your layout.

TOTAL TIME TO SCRAPLIFT:

## 30
minutes

### from the pantry

- ☐ 4 sheets of cardstock

- ☐ 2 strips of patterned paper (striped)

- ☐ 2 sheets of letter stickers

- ☐ 1 piece of ribbon

- ☐ 1 pen

- ☐ 7 photographs **4×6**

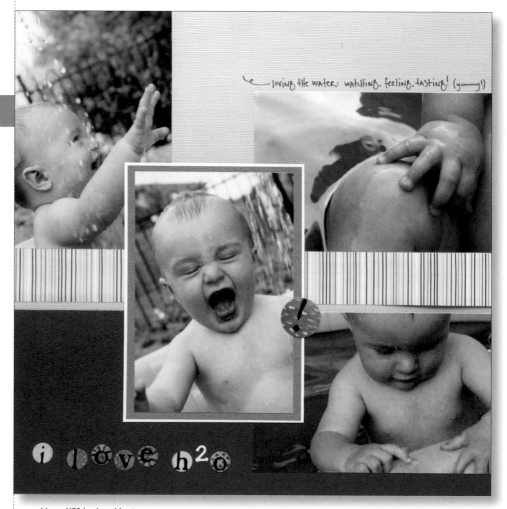

**I Love H20** by Amy Montgomery
**Supplies** *Textured cardstock:* Bazzill Basics Paper; *Patterned paper:* KI Memories; *Letter stickers:* Memories Complete and Making Memories; *Pen:* Pigma Micron, Sakura; *Ribbon:* Making Memories.

## INSTRUCTIONS

1 Choose two cardstock colors to use as your background pages. Cut the other two sheets to 4½" x 12". Place one piece on the bottom of the left page and the other on the top of the right page.

2 Place a strip of patterned paper slightly above the 4½" x 12" cardstock piece on the left page

and slightly below the 4½" x 12" cardstock piece on the right page.

3 Mat two photos and adhere all of the photos to the layout. Handwrite your journaling, and apply stickers to create the title.

# 1
## hour

## from the pantry

☐ 5 sheets of cardstock

☐ 6 strips of patterned paper
(geometric)

☐ 5 pieces of ribbon

☐ 1 sheet of number stickers

☐ 2 sheets of rub-on letters

☐ 1 pen

☐ 1 inkpad

☐ 6 photographs

## make it (even) easier!

Use coordinating patterned
papers and embellishments
to take the guesswork out
of mixing supplies.

**4 Years** by Dece Gheradini
**Supplies** *Textured cardstock and stamping ink:* Bazzill Basics Paper; *Patterned papers:* Michael Miller Memories and Scrapworks; *Rub-ons:* Doodlebug Design and KI Memories; *Ribbon:* American Crafts; *Pen:* Pigma Micron, Sakura.

## INSTRUCTIONS

1 Double mat your focal-point photos and adhere them to the layout.

2 Cut strips of paper to place underneath the other photos and to use as page accents. Ink the edges, tie ribbons around a few of them, then adhere them to the layout.

3 Adhere your photos to the layout, apply stickers and rub-ons to create your title, and handwrite the date.

## 20 minutes

### from the pantry

☐ 1 sheet of cardstock

☐ 4 strips of patterned paper (2 floral, 2 textured)

☐ 1 set of letter stamps

☐ 1 inkpad

☐ 1 pen

☐ 4 photographs

## make it (even) easier!

Instead of trimming three photos to fill the left-hand side of the photo block, use one photo and an additional (or larger) piece of patterned paper.

**Early Snow** by Nicole Gartland
**Supplies** *Patterned papers:* Wordsworth (orange), Hot Off The Press (snowflake) and K&Company (pink and green); *Letter stamps:* Technique Tuesday; *Pen:* Pigma Micron, Sakura; *Stamping ink:* ColorBox, Clearsnap.

## INSTRUCTIONS

1  Stamp the title and write your journaling directly on the top portion of the page.

2  Adhere a photo to the lower-left corner of a large strip of patterned paper. Attach this block directly to the right-hand side of the page. Group your remaining photos into a single block and place it on the left side of the page.

3  Cut three strips of paper: two ½" x 12" strips and one ¾" x 8" strip. Arrange these strips to create a blocked photo space.

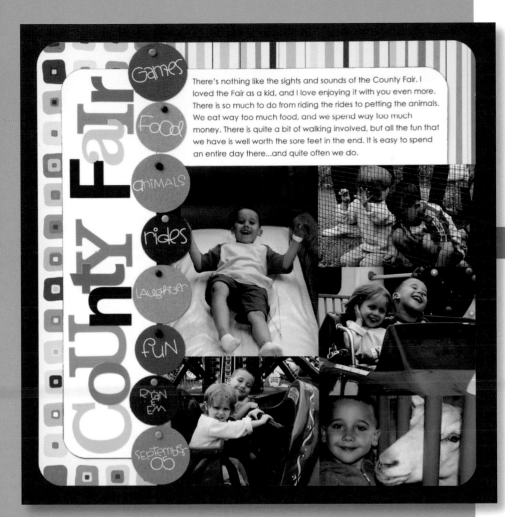

County Fair by Denine Zielinski
**Supplies** *Textured cardstock:* Bazzill Basics Paper; *Patterned papers:* KI Memories; *Rub-ons:* Doodlebug Design; *Corner rounder:* EK Success; *Circle punches:* Marvy Uchida; *Letter stickers and mini brads:* Making Memories; *Computer font:* Century Gothic, Microsoft Word.

TOTAL TIME TO SCRAPLIFT:

1 hour

## from the pantry

- ☐ 2 sheets of cardstock
- ☐ 2 strips of patterned paper (1 geometric, 1 striped)
- ☐ 2 circle punches (1 large, 1 small)
- ☐ 1 corner rounder punch
- ☐ 1 sheet of rub-on letters
- ☐ 1 sheet of letter stickers
- ☐ 8 mini brads
- ☐ 1 computer font
- ☐ 5 photographs

## INSTRUCTIONS

1 Group photos together to create an 8" x 8" photo block. Place the block in the lower-right corner of the layout.

2 Round the outside corners of the patterned paper strips and place them to the left and to the top of the photo block. Adhere your printed journaling over the patterned-paper.

3 Add the title using letter stickers. Create a page border using two sizes and four colors of punched circles. Attach them to your page with mini brads and embellish with rub-on words.

## make it (even) easier!

Use your own handwriting instead of computer-journaling Replace the rub-on words with your own handwriting.

## 45
minutes

### from the pantry

- ☐ 4 sheets of cardstock
- ☐ 1 sheet of patterned paper (striped)
- ☐ 1 sheet of letter stickers
- ☐ 2 pens
- ☐ 6 photographs 4×6

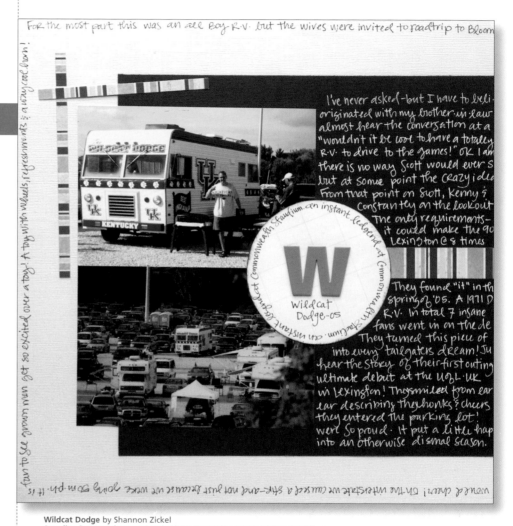

**Wildcat Dodge** by Shannon Zickel
**Supplies** *Patterned paper:* Scenic Route Paper Co.; *Letter sticker:* Heidi Swapp for Advantus; *Pens:* Pigment Pro, American Crafts.

## INSTRUCTIONS

1 Attach a piece of cardstock to your layout. Adhere three-fourths of it to the left page and one-fourth to the right page.

2 Arrange your photos on the page. Cut a circle and place a letter sticker in the center of it. Write around the edges of the circle and the edges of the layout.

3 Handwrite your journaling and embellish the page with strips of patterned paper.

# 30
## minutes

## from the pantry

- ☐ 3 sheets of cardstock
- ☐ 3 sheets of patterned paper (1 floral, 1 geometric, 1 striped)
- ☐ 1 sheet of letter stickers
- ☐ 1 sheet of number stickers
- ☐ 3 pieces of ribbon
- ☐ 7 brads
- ☐ 1 pen
- ☐ 9 photographs

## make it (even) easier!

Use just one patterned paper rather than color-blocking the layout with three designs.

*who could have guessed how much fun a group of seven & eight year old party-goers could have with a couple dozen cupcakes and a table full of candy & frosting?! Everyone had a blast creating their own unique pieces of edible art!!*

**Cupcakes** by Wendy Sue Anderson
**Supplies** *Patterned papers:* The C-Thru Ruler Co.; *Letter stickers:* American Crafts; *Number stickers:* Chatterbox; *Ribbon:* Making Memories (yellow), C.M. Offray & Son (orange) and American Crafts (red); *Pen:* Zig Writer, EK Success; *Brads:* Making Memories.

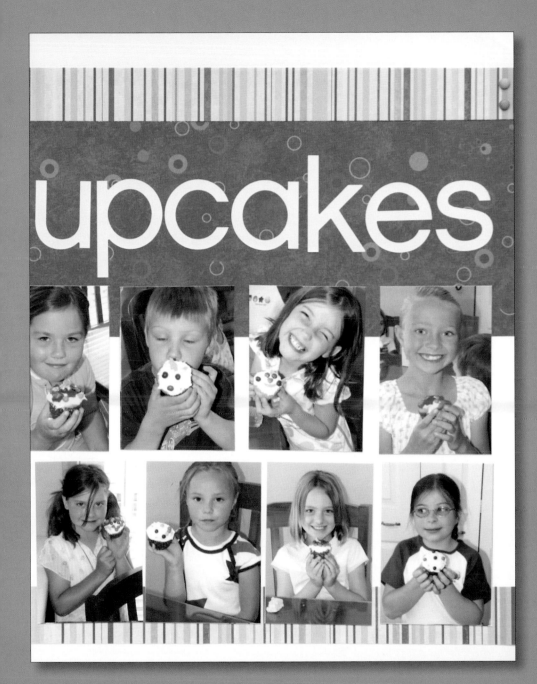

## INSTRUCTIONS

1 Cut patterned papers to color-block a white cardstock background.

2 Mat your focal-point photo and trim the rest to fit. Arrange them on your page.

3 Apply stickers to create your title, and handwrite your journaling. Embellish your page with ribbon and brads.

# 1
## hour

## from the pantry

☐ 4 sheets of cardstock

☐ 3 sheets of patterned paper
(geometric)

☐ 1 computer font

☐ 2 sheets of letter stickers

☐ 2 sheets of rub-on letters/
numbers

☐ 5 photographs

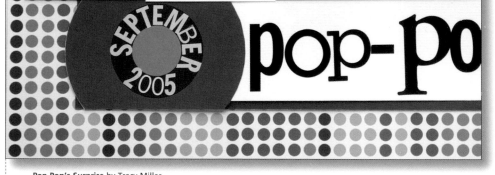

We had a surprise party for Pop-pop's 70th birthday. Except for spotting Hans just seconds before we yelled "surprise!" things went off without a hitch.

The party was at Amy's house and typical for a Miller party, there was plenty of food! Everyone was able to be there, with the exception of Uncle Kelly who was on his way to New Orleans to help the hurricane victims. We celebrated John's birthday as well.

Pop-pop got lots of good gifts, including a hat that he had been coveting. All of the children went together for his big gift – a new grill. The better to feed all of us at the next Miller family get together.

SEPTEMBER 2005

pop-po

**Pop-Pop's Surprise** by Tracy Miller
**Supplies** *Patterned papers:* SEI; *Letter stickers:* American Crafts ("Pop-Pop") and Scrapworks ("Surprise"); *Rub-ons:* Scrapworks; *Computer font:* Arial, Microsoft Word.

## INSTRUCTIONS

1 Trim the white cardstock, mat it with red cardstock and mount it onto your patterned-paper background.

2 Line up your photos, leaving space for your journaling. Create your title with letter stickers. Print your journaling and attach it to the layout.

3 Cut circles from patterned paper and adhere them to the layout, layering them over or under other elements. Use rub-ons for the date and page accents.

TOTAL TIME TO SCRAPLIFT:

## 20
minutes

### from the pantry

- ☐ 3 sheets of cardstock
- ☐ 2 strips of patterned paper (1 floral, 1 striped)
- ☐ 3 staples
- ☐ 1 sheet of letter stickers
- ☐ 1 pen
- ☐ 3 photographs 4×6

**Silly** by Wendy Sue Anderson
**Supplies** *Patterned papers:* Crate Paper; *Letter stickers and staples:* Making Memories; *Pen:* Zig Writer, EK Success.

## make it (even) easier!

This page is already so simple and quick, but you can make it even easier by not matting the photo.

## INSTRUCTIONS

**1** Cut strips of patterned paper and card-stock and adhere them to the left edge of the layout.

**2** Mat your focal-point photo and adhere all three photos to the layout. Cut two photo corners from cardstock and place them on the right page to emphasize your photos.

**3** Handwrite your journaling on strips of green cardstock and staple them to the layout. Apply letter stickers to create your title.

# 30
## minutes

## from the pantry

- ☐ 2 sheets of cardstock

- ☐ 2 sheets of patterned paper
  (1 geometric, 1 striped)

- ☐ 1 pen

- ☐ 3 sheets of letter stickers

- ☐ 2 punctuation marks/dingbats
  from sheet of letter stickers

- ☐ 1 brad

- ☐ 2 pieces of ribbon

- ☐ 2 staples

- ☐ 5 photographs

## make it
## (even) easier!

Print your journaling on a
block of cardstock, leaving
open space for your title.

**Go Cards** by Shannon Zickel
**Supplies** *Patterned papers:* KI Memories; *Letter stickers:* Scrapworks, American
Crafts and Making Memories; *Brad:* Making Memories; *Pen:* Pigment Pro,
American Crafts; *Other:* Ribbon.

The journaling reads:

's had season tickets to UK football for a few YEARS - so I wasn't
hen we had the chance to get some fairly decent and very
season tickets for the UofL games - if he would want to or not -
realizing there were very few schedule conflicts - we went
what a great season it was! We loved spending our Saturday
S together - tailgating and having fun! The cards went 9-3 for
You became a true football fan - and gained an
on for the game. You were interested in learning the
the thing I was most excited about was that You
true Cardinal Fan!
have Daddy out -
I've got a partner
es time to take sides
UofL games. Now that
g to cheer about!

**go caRDS**

a Saturday in fall 2003

## INSTRUCTIONS

1 Trim four horizontal 4" x 6" photos to span both pages of your layout. Line them up 1½" from the top of the layout and adhere them to the cardstock.

2 Attach a square of patterned paper to the lower-left corner of the layout. Attach a strip of patterned paper across the top and bottom of the layout.

3 Staple ribbon to your focal-point photo and adhere it to the layout. Handwrite your journaling and add letter stickers to create your title.

**1 hour**

## from the pantry

- ☐ 6 sheets of cardstock
- ☐ 1 sheet of patterned paper (geometric)
- ☐ 2 pieces of ribbon
- ☐ 1 inkpad
- ☐ 1 set of letter stamps
- ☐ 1 pen
- ☐ 1 computer font
- ☐ 1 sheet of letter stickers
- ☐ 1 sheet of number stickers
- ☐ 4 circle punches (various sizes)
- ☐ 4 photographs 4×6

**Burger King Birthday** by Tarri Botwinski
**Supplies** *Textured cardstock:* Bazzill Basics Paper; *Patterned paper:* Scenic Route Paper; *Letter stamps:* Making Memories; *Stamping ink:* ColorBox, Clearsnap; *Number sticker:* American Crafts; *Ribbon:* C.M. Offray & Son; *Letter stickers:* Die Cuts With a View; *Circle punches and pen:* Marvy Uchida; *Computer font:* Century Gothic, Microsoft Word.

**INSTRUCTIONS**

1 Cut two large strips of patterned paper and adhere them to the bottom of the layout. Layer ribbon over the strips. Mat a small strip of patterned paper and adhere it to the top center of the layout.

2 Place a number sticker over several circle punches, layering them to create an accent. Mat your photos and journaling block and adhere them to your layout.

3 Stamp your title, then trace around the letters with a pen. Finish your title by applying letter stickers to the top corners of the layout.

TOTAL TIME TO SCRAPLIFT:

## 45 minutes

### from the pantry

☐ 2 sheets of cardstock

☐ 1 sheet of patterned paper (striped)

☐ 5 pieces of rickrack

☐ 3 paper clips

☐ 2 staples

☐ 1 sheet of letter stickers with accents

☐ 1 sheet of rub-on letters/ numbers

☐ 1 pen

☐ 4 photo corners

☐ 5 photographs

## make it (even) easier!

Just skip Step 3—
don't add the paper
clips with ribbon and the
photo corners on the
bottom photos.

**Dizzy Day** by Wendy Sue Anderson
**Supplies** *Textured cardstock: patterned paper, rickrack, rub-on letters, letter stickers, flower accents and staples: Making Memories; Photo corners: Lineco; Paper clips: OfficeMax; Pen: Zig Writer, EK Success.*

## INSTRUCTIONS

1 Attach a strip of patterned paper to the bottom portion of the page. Add letter stickers to the upper-right corner of the page to create your title.

2 Mat your photos (one full size and four trimmed) on cardstock and arrange them on the page. Create a pull-out journaling tab using cardstock and a strip of patterned paper and stapling rickrack to the edge.

3 Tie ribbon on paper clips and attach them to three photos. Create a date tab by applying rub-ons to a scrap of patterned paper. Staple a ribbon to embellish it.

2. Oktober 1997
Munich Germany
My whole Stockwerk decided to head over to the biggest tourist trap in Southern Germany, so with Kim in tow, I went along for (what I believed) was a one-time opportunity to meet people of all ages and nationalities and drink and dance on tables... By the end of the evening, after a Maß and a half (to this day don't know where that second Maß came from, have a sinking suspicion, I just picked it up off the table...the only people left of our group were Kim, myself, a guy we called 'Doc' and his neighbor. Unfortunately, Doc turned out to be violent when drunk and picked a fight at the U-bahn. He got his glasses knocked off him and a bloody nose and his poor neighbor had to drag him out of it and flag down a taxi alone as he was too intoxicated to understand what he was doing! Kim proceeded to spend the night in my room, as she had to catch a train to an early conference the next morning. It was definitely a one-time experience, although I visited Oktoberfest for the next two proceeding years before boycotting the place all together!

PROST!

KIM & Amber

**Oktoberfest** by Amber Ries
**Supplies** *Patterned papers:* Wordsworth and KI Memories; *Ribbon:* Making Memories; *Photo turns:* 7gypsies; *Pen:* Zig Writer, EK Success; *Computer fonts:* Arial, Microsoft Word; CK Chemistry, "Fresh Fonts" CD, *Creating Keepsakes; Other:* Mini brads.

TOTAL TIME TO SCRAPLIFT:

## 45 minutes

## from the pantry

☐ 2 sheets of cardstock

☐ 2 sheets of patterned paper (textured)

☐ 2 computer fonts

☐ 1 pen

☐ 2 photo turns

☐ 2 mini brads

☐ 1 piece of ribbon

☐ 3 photographs

## INSTRUCTIONS

1 Adhere a 5" strip of patterned paper to the left side of the page. Arrange three photos on the page.

2 Cut out your title and adhere it to your background paper. Send the whole thing through the printer to add your journaling on top of the title. Trim and adhere it to your layout.

3 Separate the journaling from the photos with a ribbon border; add photo turns and descriptive tags.

## make it (even) easier!

Instead of hand-cutting your title, adhere letter stickers or rub-ons to a strip of cardstock and run the strip through your printer to add journaling.

TOTAL TIME TO SCRAPLIFT:

## 30 minutes

### from the pantry

- ☐ 4 sheets of cardstock
- ☐ 1 sheet of patterned paper (floral)
- ☐ 2 pens
- ☐ 1 sheet of letter stickers
- ☐ 6 photographs  4×6

## INSTRUCTIONS

**1** After attaching the photos to the cardstock, fill in the spaces between the photos with patterned paper.

**2** Cut several thin strips of peach-colored cardstock and attach them between and around the photos.

**3** Place a letter-sticker title underneath the photo block. Cut up your handwritten journaling and line up the words along the top of the photo block and below your title.

**Red Rock Adventure** by Mimi Schramm
**Supplies** *Textured cardstock:* Bazzill Basics Paper; *Patterned paper:* Scenic Route Paper Co.; *Letter stickers:* American Crafts; *Pens:* Le Plume (black), Marvy Uchida; Uni-ball Signo (white), Sanford.

## make it (even) easier!

Instead of cutting your journaling into little word boxes, just write it directly on the black cardstock using a white gel pen.

## 30 minutes

**La Serie de Cercle** by Moon Ko
**Supplies** *Textured cardstock:* Michaels; *Patterned paper:* Pieces of Me; *Brads:* Making Memories; *Computer fonts:* PegsannaHMK, Book Antiqua and Engravers MT, downloaded from the Internet; *Other:* Date stamp.

## from the pantry

- ☐ 2 sheets of cardstock
- ☐ 1 strip of patterned paper (geometric)
- ☐ 2 brads
- ☐ 2 computer fonts
- ☐ 4 scans of artwork
- ☐ 1 date stamp
- ☐ 1 photograph  **4×6**

## INSTRUCTIONS

1 Cut the artwork into strips and mat them with black cardstock. After adhering the artwork to your page, place your photo in the open space on the left.

2 Adhere a strip of patterned paper along the bottom edge of the page.

3 Affix your title strip with brads, and your caption labels with glue.

## make it (even) easier!

Feature one larger piece of artwork by your child (instead of four).

TOTAL TIME TO SCRAPLIFT:

## 45
minutes

- ☐ 4 sheets of cardstock
- ☐ 1 strip of patterned paper (geometric)
- ☐ 2 sheets of rub-on letters
- ☐ 5 brads
- ☐ 1 piece of ribbon
- ☐ 4 circle punches (various sizes)
- ☐ 4 photo corners
- ☐ 7 photographs
- ☐ 1 computer font

### INSTRUCTIONS

1  Arrange your photos on the layout.

2  Use various sizes of circle punches (or hole punches) to punch circle designs into a strip of ribbon and a small square of cardstock. Mat the ribbon with a strip of patterned paper and adhere it to your layout.

3  Adhere your printed journaling to the page, apply rub-on letters to create your title, and accent your page with brads.

man ...

...you and daddy did a great job building our first snowman! It was New Year's Day and the snow was perfect for packing so we raced outside to play. I was surprised at how much you liked it outside in the cold... you didn't even mind when you got a bit of snow in your face! The snowman was pretty funny with his carrot nose and corncob pipe, but you thought it was even funnier the next day when you looked out the window and saw his head was "all gone".

**Snowman** by Amy Montgomery
**Supplies** *Textured cardstock:* Bazzill Basics Paper; *Patterned paper:* BasicGrey; *Rub-ons, brads and circle punches:* Making Memories; *Computer font:* Century Gothic, downloaded from the Internet; *Other:* Ribbon.

## make it (even) easier!

Instead of punching out a circle design on a strip of ribbon or cardstock, choose a second patterned paper to serve as an accent strip.

**Supplies** *Textured cardstock:* Die Cuts With a View; *Patterned papers:* Déjà Views by The C-Thru Ruler Co. (red) and Chloe's Closet (black), Imagination Project; *Brads:* All My Memories.

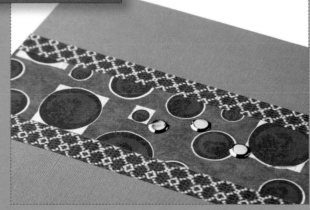

TOTAL TIME TO SCRAPLIFT:

## 25
minutes

### from the pantry

☐  2 sheets of cardstock

☐  1 strip of patterned paper
    (geometric)

☐  1 piece of ribbon

☐  1 sheet of rub-on letters

☐  1 brad

☐  1 pen

☐  1 computer font

☐  1 photograph

**E-Mail @ Paradise** by Laura Kurz
**Supplies** *Patterned paper:* KI Memories; *Rub-on letters:* Scrapworks; *Ribbon:* SEI; *Computer font ("@"):* Arial, Microsoft Word; *Other:* Brad and pen.

## INSTRUCTIONS

1   Adhere a strip of patterned paper across the middle of the page. Affix a strip of cardstock directly underneath the patterned-paper strip.

2   Hide the divide between the two papers with a strip of ribbon. Attach the ribbon with a decorative brad.

3   Print out part of your title and use rub-on letters to finish. Adhere your photo and handwrite your journaling.

Europe by Traci Turchin
**Supplies** *Textured cardstock:* Bazzill Basics Paper; *Pen:* Pigment Pro, American Crafts; *Computer font:* Univers, downloaded from *www.linotype.com*.

TOTAL TIME TO SCRAPLIFT:

## 30 minutes

### from the pantry

☐ 2 sheets of cardstock

☐ 1 pen

☐ 1 computer font

☐ 9 photographs

## make it (even) easier!

Instead of cutting letters from photographs, simply use letter stickers to create your title.

## INSTRUCTIONS

1 Print the title on a piece of scrap paper. Cut the letters out and trace them onto your photos, then cut the letters out again. Adhere the letters to the top portion of the page.

2 Crop three photos to 3½" x 6" and line them up along the bottom of the page.

3 Handwrite your journaling around the block of three photos.

**Supplies** *Textured cardstock:* Hot Off The Press; *Letter stickers:* K&Company.

# the pantry + 1

Now and then, a special dish requires an ingredient you don't typically keep on hand. But if the entrée is tasty, it's worth picking it up. With just one extra item, you can create these delectable layouts!

TOTAL TIME TO SCRAPLIFT:

## 20
minutes

### from the pantry

☐  2 sheets cardstock

☐  1 sheet patterned paper

☐  1 set letter stickers

☐  1 computer font

☐  4 photographs

### just add

☐  3 rhinestones

**So Pretty** by Angela Hancock. **Supplies** *Software:* Adobe Photoshop CS2; *Cardstock:* Bazzill Basics Paper; *Patterned paper:* BasicGrey; *Acrylic letters:* Heidi Swapp for Advantus; *Rhinestones:* K&Company; *Butterfly punch:* Martha Stewart Crafts; *Font:* Avant Garde.

## make it
## (even) easier!

Use two 4" x 6" photos instead
of four cropped photos.

...so

Pretty

You two are so adorable together. You are so different and so alike at the same time. Bella is such a free spirit always singing and dancing. You are always observing her. You try to be all grown up when you play together. Today when Bella came over you had such fun. You both wanted me to take your pictures. I didn't want to pass up this opportunity since usually you are not willing to let me snap away until my heart is content. Today was different. You were carefree and enjoyed our little photo shoot. I ended up getting so many adorable photos of the two of you!                    September 6, 2008

## INSTRUCTIONS

1 Type journaling using computer and print on cardstock.

2 Trim photos and adhere to cardstock.

3 Add strip of paper, title, rhinestones and punched butterfly accent.

TOTAL TIME TO SCRAPLIFT:

## 45 minutes

### from the pantry

- ☐ 3 sheets cardstock (1 laser-cut)
- ☐ 1 sheet specialty paper (red leather)
- ☐ 3 strips patterned paper (striped)
- ☐ 8 foam sticker accents
- ☐ 7 brads
- ☐ Embroidery floss
- ☐ 1 computer font
- ☐ 6 photographs

### just add

- ☐ 1 tube dimensional paint

## make it (even) easier!

Use a white pen to add dots instead of using dimensional paint.

**Jonny's Super Cool Day with the Best Aunts Ever!** by Susan Opel. **Supplies** *Cardstock:* Bazzill Basics Paper (white) and KI Memories (black laser-cut); *Patterned paper:* Fibermark (red leather) and KI Memories (striped); *Foam accents:* KI Memories; *Brad:* Creative Impressions; *Dimensional paint:* Liquid Appliqué, Marvy Uchida; *Font:* Century Gothic.

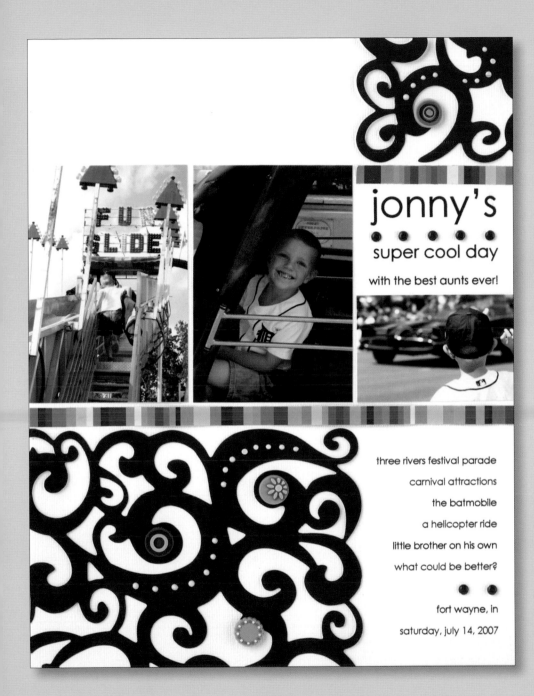

jonny's
super cool day
with the best aunts ever!

three rivers festival parade
carnival attractions
the batmobile
a helicopter ride
little brother on his own
what could be better?

fort wayne, in
saturday, july 14, 2007

## INSTRUCTIONS

1 Print title and journaling on background paper, leaving room between for photo. Crop six vertical photos to the same width, cropping one photo to half the height of the others. Adhere in a line above center of layout.

2 Apply thin strip of striped paper under photos and above title and rectangle of red paper to lower left of layout. Add sections of laser-cut swirl paper to bottom-center and top-right.

3 Attach swirl accent to top left. Add dots to paper with dimensional paint. Finish with brads and foam embellishments.

TOTAL TIME TO SCRAPLIFT:

## 30 minutes

### from the pantry

- ☐ 3 sheets cardstock
- ☐ 4 sheets patterned paper (dot, star, red grid and blue grid)
- ☐ 2 sets letter stickers
- ☐ 5 word stickers
- ☐ 3 die-cut stickers
- ☐ 1 rub-on sentiment
- ☐ 1 inkpad
- ☐ 1 computer font
- ☐ 5 photographs 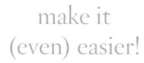 4×6

### just add

- ☐ 1 transparency frame

## make it (even) easier!

If your papers stand out from the background enough, inking may not be necessary.

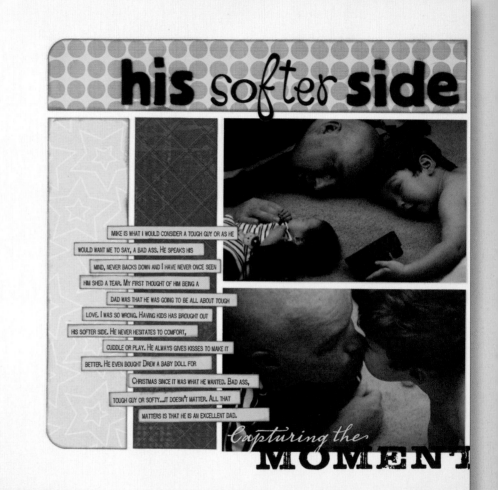

**His Softer Side** by Allison Davis. **Supplies** *Cardstock:* Bazzill Basics Paper; *Patterned paper:* KI Memories (yellow) and Scenic Route (orange, blue and green); *Letter stickers:* American Crafts ("His" and "Side") and Doodlebug Design ("Softer"); *Word stickers:* 7gypsies ("Smile" and "Kids"), K&Company ("Fun!" and "Too Sweet") and Making Memories ("Family"); *Die-cut stickers:* Daisy D's Paper Co. (quote card) and My Mind's Eye ("Memories" and "Together"); *Transparency:* Rusty Pickle; *Ink:* ColorBox Fluid Chalk, Clearsnap; *Font:* AL Old Remington; *Other:* Corner-rounder punch and rub-on sentiment.

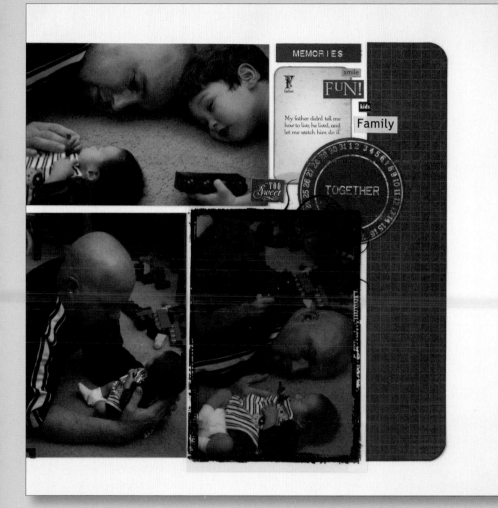

## INSTRUCTIONS

1 Arrange photos on cardstock, leaving small margins between them. Cut 2"-wide strips of several papers and arrange with photos to create rectangle block. Round rectangle corners, ink edges and apply to layout.

2 Create journaling on computer and cut into strips. Apply to layout. Attach title.

3 Add die cuts, stickers and rub-on sentiment. Emphasize one photo with transparency frame.

## 30 minutes

### from the pantry

- ☐ 4 sheets cardstock (1 scallop-edged)
- ☐ 1 sheet patterned paper (striped)
- ☐ 2 sets letter stickers
- ☐ 1 journaling stamp
- ☐ 1 chipboard heart
- ☐ 1 inkpad
- ☐ 1 rub-on word
- ☐ 1 label sticker
- ☐ Embroidery floss
- ☐ 1 pen
- ☐ 3 photographs  4×6

### just add

- ☐ 1 set letter die cuts

### make it (even) easier!

Use a border sticker instead of
the scalloped cardstock.

**Leaf Throwing Dance** by Ruth Dealey. **Supplies** *Cardstock and scallop-edged cardstock:* Bazzill Basics Paper; *Patterned paper, letter stickers, letter die cuts and chipboard heart:* BasicGrey; *Stamp:* Autumn Leaves; *Ink:* Stampin' Up!; *Pen:* Uni-ball Signo, Newell Rubbermaid; *Other:* Label sticker, embroidery floss, scallop-edged scissors and rub-on word.

### INSTRUCTIONS

1. Trim white cardstock and adhere to red cardstock background. Line up three vertical photos toward bottom of page. Add strip of patterned paper and scalloped cardstock.

2. Stamp on brown cardstock and journal with white pen. Mat with orange cardstock cut with scalloped-edged scissors and attach to layout. Apply letter stickers for title.

3. Apply rub-on word to label. Add chipboard heart and attach to layout.

**The Sweet Life** by Grace Tolman. **Supplies** *Cardstock:* Die Cuts With a View; *Patterned paper:* Creative Café and Creative Imaginations; *Chipboard letter stickers:* Heidi Swapp for Advantus; *Chipboard bookplate:* Grungeboard, Ranger Industries; *Stamp:* KI Memories; *Die-cut machine:* Cuttlebug, Provo Craft; *Paint:* Plaid Enterprises; *Adhesive:* Elmer's; *Other:* Corner-rounder punch, border-sticker strip and brads.

## from the pantry

- ☐ 1 sheet cardstock
- ☐ 2 sheets patterned paper (small dot and larger dot)
- ☐ 1 set chipboard letter stickers
- ☐ 1 chipboard bookplate
- ☐ 1 tube paint
- ☐ 1 set letter stamps
- ☐ 1 inkpad
- ☐ 1 border-sticker strip
- ☐ 2 brads
- ☐ 1 computer font
- ☐ 3 photographs 4×6

## just add

- ☐ Die-cut heart accents

## INSTRUCTIONS

1 Attach three horizontal photos in a column toward left edge of patterned paper. Add border strip to left side of photos. Cut two rectangles of even width but different heights out of a coordinating paper. Round outer corners and attach to right of photos.

2 Stamp word on cardstock and enclose in bookplate. Attach to layout with brads. Create heart accents with die-cut machine.

3 Print journaling and cut out, inking edges before adding to layout. Finish with painted chipboard title.

## make it (even) easier!

Don't have all the letters you need? Get creative! The two e's in Sweet are actually 3s, and the f was originally a p.

## 30 minutes

### from the pantry

- ☐ 2 sheets cardstock

- ☐ 4 sheets patterned paper (teal, diamond, dot and floral)

- ☐ 3 sets letter stickers

- ☐ 2 word stickers

- ☐ 2 chipboard hearts

- ☐ 1 yard ribbon

- ☐ Thread

- ☐ 1 pen

- ☐ 9 photographs

### just add

- ☐ 1 notebook label die cut

## make it (even) easier!

No ribbon? Cardstock or patterned paper makes a great substitute.

**We Are a Family That Loves Nature** by Jennifer Davis. **Supplies** *Cardstock:* Bazzill Basics Paper; *Patterned paper:* Jenni Bowlin Studio and October Afternoon; *Ribbon:* Making Memories; *Letter stickers:* American Crafts (large brown) and Pink Paislee (small brown); *Word stickers:* Bookworks, EK Success; *Pen:* American Crafts; *Adhesive:* Kokuyo and Making Memories (ribbon glue); *Other:* Thread, green letter stickers, chipboard hearts and notebook label die cut.

### INSTRUCTIONS

1 Crop all photos to 4" tall. Arrange on cardstock and adhere. Add patterned paper in strips and rectangles.

2 Write journaling on notebook label die cut and adhere. Create title with letter stickers, word stickers and chipboard hearts.

3 Machine-stitch ribbon to layout as desired.

## bonus project

Jennifer used the reverse side of her patterned-paper scraps and made this groovy card!

**You Are the Cat's Meow** by Jennifer Davis. **Supplies** *Cardstock:* Bazzill Basics Paper; *Patterned paper:* October Afternoon; *Word stickers:* Bookworks, EK Success; *Stamp:* Technique Tuesday; *Punches:* Fiskars (circle) and Marvy Uchida (scallop); *Ribbon:* May Arts; *Other:* Thread.

TOTAL TIME TO SCRAPLIFT:

## 30 minutes

### from the pantry

- ☐ 5 sheets cardstock
- ☐ 4 sheets patterned paper (various blues)
- ☐ 1 set letter stickers
- ☐ 1 foam sticker (airplane)
- ☐ 12 epoxy stickers
- ☐ Thread
- ☐ 1 computer font
- ☐ 4 photographs

### just add

- ☐ 15 buttons

My flight departed so early (6 a.m.!!!) and O'Hare, which is normally so busy, was calm and quiet. I stopped and grabbed some breakfast before heading to the gate.

I was able to get a window seat in an empty row of two all by myself. So nice. The flight was incredibly relaxing, I just sat back and slept most of the time. The flight attendants kept us well fed with boxes full of snacks and cans of pop anytime.

**Up, Up and Away** by Kelly Purkey. **Supplies** *Cardstock, letter stickers and foam airplane sticker:* American Crafts; *Patterned paper:* American Crafts (light-blue swirls), KI Memories (dark-blue swirls) and Li'l Davis Designs (light-blue and dark-blue crosshatch); *Epoxy stickers:* Cloud 9 Design, Fiskars; *Buttons:* Li'l Davis Designs; *Corner-rounder punch:* Fiskars; *Font:* AL Uncle Charles; *Other:* Thread.

## make it (even) easier!

Forego the sewing and just glue down the buttons.

**up, up, and away**

Even though I'd done a Trans-Atlantic flight before, I definitely didn't remember the plane being that BIG. I was amazed by how nice the first class was as I made my way back to coach. It was cool how wide the plane was with 3 seats in the middle.

Just a bit before we landed it was time for dinner. I really wasn't expecting much from airline food but it was great. Little things like how each of the foods had their own little compartment amuse me. Dinner + watching Greys was a perfect ending.

## INSTRUCTIONS

1 Mat four 11½" x 5¼" pieces of patterned paper on various shades of 12" x 6" blue cardstock, rounding top corners. Trim four horizontal photos and attach.

2 Create journaling on computer, cut in strips and attach to layout. Add letter stickers for title.

3 Sew on buttons in swirl formation. Finish with airplane and epoxy stickers.

TOTAL TIME TO SCRAPLIFT:

# 30
## minutes

## from the pantry

☐ 5 sheets cardstock

☐ 2 sheets patterned paper
  (diamond and striped)

☐ 1 set rub-on letters

☐ 1 chipboard flower accent

☐ 3 brads

☐ Thread

☐ 2 computer fonts

☐ 5 photographs

## just add

☐ 3 eyelets

**Cousins Cruising the Neighborhood** by Sheri Reguly. **Supplies** *Cardstock:* Bazzill Basics Paper; *Patterned paper:* October Afternoon; *Chipboard flower accent:* KI Memories; *Brads:* Doodlebug Design; *Eyelets:* Making Memories; *Circle punch:* Marvy Uchida; *Fonts:* Bickley Script (title) and Times New Roman (journaling); *Other:* Thread.

## make it
## (even) easier!

Create your title with
stickers or rub-ons.

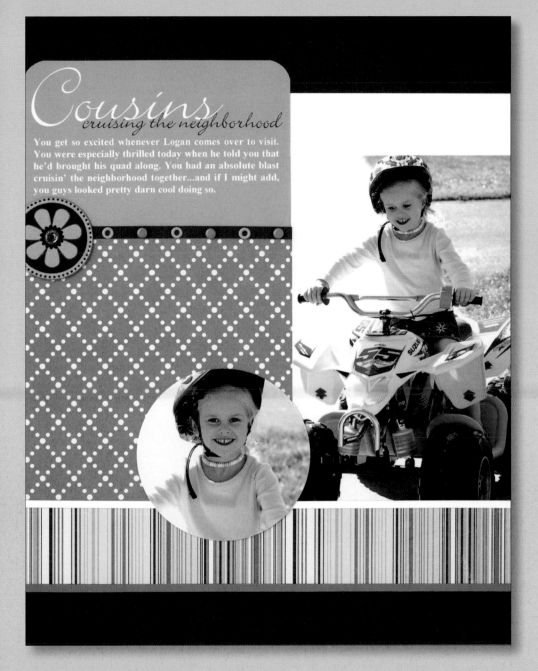

## Cousins
### cruising the neighborhood

You get so excited whenever Logan comes over to visit. You were especially thrilled today when he told you that he'd brought his quad along. You had an absolute blast cruisin' the neighborhood together...and if I might add, you guys looked pretty darn cool doing so.

## INSTRUCTIONS

1 Apply strips of dark cardstock to top and bottom of two-page white background. Mount two 4"-wide photos on left and one on far right in a line slightly above center. Add striped strip and thin blue strip beneath photos.

2 Create title and journaling block on computer and attach to patterned-paper rectangle. Add brown strip where papers meet and embellish with eyelets and brads. Sew down chipboard flower accent.

3 Overlap striped strip with one cropped 4" wide photo. Punch additional photo out with circle punch and apply.

TOTAL TIME TO SCRAPLIFT:

## 45
minutes

## from the pantry

- ☐ 2 sheets cardstock

- ☐ 5 sheets patterned paper
  (striped, plaid and 3 dot)

- ☐ 2 sets letter stickers

- ☐ 4 chipboard accents

- ☐ 1 tube paint

- ☐ Several word stickers

- ☐ 1 sheet rub-ons

- ☐ 1 inkpad

- ☐ 1 computer font

- ☐ 3 photographs 4×6

## just add

- ☐ 1 set chipboard letters

## make it
## (even) easier!

In a rush? Forget
the inking.

**The Big One** by Allison Davis. **Supplies** *Cardstock:* Bazzill Basics Paper; *Patterned paper:* Bo-Bunny Press (multicolor and striped) and Scenic Route (orange and blue); *Letter stickers:* American Crafts ("One") and Doodlebug Design ("The"); *Chipboard letters:* Maya Road; *Chipboard accents:* Maya Road (arrows) and me & my BIG ideas ("Warning"); *Word stickers:* 7gypsies; *Rub-ons:* Daisy D's Paper Co.; *Paint:* Making Memories; *Ink:* ColorBox Fluid Chalk, Clearsnap; *Font:* American Typewriter.

IG
one
busy
BIG BOY
oops!
joy of boys
tough
I WANT MY MOMMY
damage fallout
I knew that sooner or later Drew was going to have injuries. He is a boy after all. Skinned knees, bruises, a cut or two, maybe even a fat lip... I was expecting it. What I wasn't expecting just yet was the big one. The injury that hurt me as bad as it hurt him. He fell off the step on the back porch and landed flat on his forehead. Within seconds a huge bump had formed. As he cried and said over and over, "Mommy, it hurts really bad!" I was doing the best that I could not to cry myself. Mike thought that maybe Drew would like to see the big bump in the mirror. I knew that was not a good idea. If Drew gets anything on his face and sees it in a mirror he flips out. I knew that he would see the bump and want us to get it off. I was right. The rest of the evening was spent comforting Drew. The big injuries... I'm so not ready for this!
WARNING:
DON'T TRY
THIS AT
HOME
no whiners allowed
rough

## INSTRUCTIONS

1. Type journaling and print on dot paper. Cut out blocks of three different dot papers (including journaling section) and strip of striped paper. Ink edges of papers.

2. Arrange photos and blocks on white cardstock. Before adhering, round outer corners of bottom two papers and place striped paper strip beneath bottom photo.

3. Add various rub-ons and stickers as embellishments. Combine letter stickers for title.

1 hour

## from the pantry

- ☐ 6 sheets cardstock
- ☐ 1 set letter stickers
- ☐ 5 dimensional snowflake stickers
- ☐ ½ yard ribbon (brown and red)
- ☐ 1 pen
- ☐ 1 computer font
- ☐ 4 photographs

## just add

- ☐ Several hexagon die cuts

### INSTRUCTIONS

1 Create background by cutting hexagon shapes with die-cut machine and adhering in a grid pattern.

2 Outline each photo with pen and mat on black cardstock. Use letter stickers for title and affix black photo/title block to background. Layer ribbons and attach beneath photos.

3 Create journaling on computer, cut into strips and attach to layout. Finish with snowflake stickers and handwritten date.

when we left the school after Meagan's program. we were greeted by a fresh layer of snow and lots of falling fluffy flakes. Of course, we had to take a few minutes to enjoy the fresh snow!

**Fresh Snow** by Wendy Sue Anderson. **Supplies** *Cardstock:* Bazzill Basics Paper; *Ribbon:* Bo-Bunny Press (brown dot) and K&Company (red); *Stickers:* Doodlebug Design (letters) and K&Company (snowflakes); *Electronic die-cut machine:* Cricut, Provo Craft; *Pen:* American Crafts; *Font:* 2Peas Favorite Things.

## make it (even) easier!

Substitute patterned paper for the background, and you can complete this design in a snap!

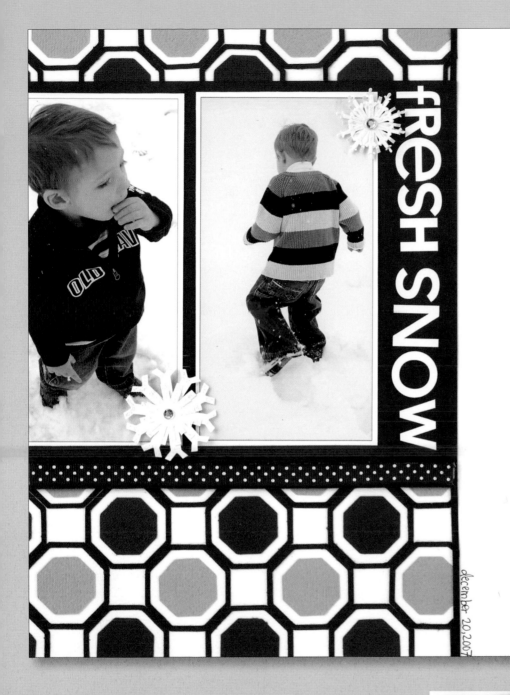

## bonus project

Wendy couldn't let her extra
hexagons go to waste, so she
whipped up this darling card!

**Hi** by Wendy Sue Anderson. **Supplies** *Card-stock: Bazzill Basics Paper (white, brown, red, teal); Ribbon: Bo-Bunny Press (red and brown dot); Rub-ons: American Crafts; Electronic die-cut machine: Cricut, Provo Craft.*

## 45
### minutes

### from the pantry

- ☐ 4 sheets cardstock
- ☐ 1 sheet patterned paper (map)
- ☐ 1 set letter stickers
- ☐ 1 inkpad
- ☐ 1 computer font
- ☐ 6 photographs

### just add

- ☐ 1 paper border

**Wild** by Courtney Kelly. **Supplies** *Cardstock:* Bazzill Basics Paper; *Patterned paper:* Collage Press; *Letter stickers:* Heidi Swapp for Advantus; *Paper border:* Doodlebug Design; *Font:* AL Highlight; *Other:* Ink.

## make it (even) easier!

Instead of inking the letter stickers, use a black marker to add a finishing touch.

AWCC

JULY 3, 2008

WARNING: THESE ANIMALS FOUND IN ALASKA, THOUGH ABUNDANT AND MAJESTIC, ARE WILD.

THEY ARE FULL OF CHARACTER, UNPREDICTABLE, AND READY FOR THEIR CLOSE-UPS.

## INSTRUCTIONS

1 Adhere black cardstock strips to top and bottom of white cardstock background. Add map paper strips to inner edge of black strips.

2 Place and attach photos. Add paper border to top and bottom of horizontal photo block.

3 Type journaling on computer, cut into strips and affix to layout. Ink letter stickers and create title.

## 45 minutes

### from the pantry

- ☐ 3 sheets cardstock
- ☐ 2 sheets patterned paper (striped and word)
- ☐ 1 rub-on title
- ☐ 1 pen
- ☐ 7 photographs

### just add

- ☐ 1 journaling spot die cut

**Gone Fishing** by Ruth Dealey. **Supplies** *Cardstock:* Bazzill Basics Paper; *Patterned paper and journaling spot:* Scenic Route; *Rub-on title:* My Mind's Eye; *Pen:* Pilot, SureSource.

## INSTRUCTIONS

1 Trim photos and create photo block. Attach to white cardstock. Add word patterned-paper strip beneath photos and apply rub-on title to bottom of paper

2 Mat white cardstock on brown background. Add blue strips along sides of photos, and striped strips at top and bottom of design.

3 Write on journaling spot and attach to layout.

## make it (even) easier!

Use a collage software program and print your photos in a single block.

## 30 minutes

**Rain Dancing** by Emilie Ahern. **Supplies** *Cardstock:* WorldWin; *Patterned paper:* American Crafts and Scenic Route; *Journaling tag die cut:* My Mind's Eye; *Scallop-edged scissors:* Fiskars; *Felt embellishment:* Tinkering Ink; *Letter stickers:* SEI; *Pen:* Zig Millennium, EK Success; *Other:* Thread and brads.

## make it (even) easier!

Have your photos printed with a border and you won't need to mat them.

## from the pantry

☐ 3 sheets cardstock

☐ 2 sheets patterned paper (grid and floral)

☐ 1 set letter stickers

☐ 1 felt embellishment

☐ 3 brads

☐ 1 pen

☐ Thread

☐ 3 photographs

## just add

☐ 1 journaling tag die cut

## INSTRUCTIONS

1 Mat grid paper on blue cardstock background. Attach patterned paper to left of center.

2 Mat two photos on coordinating colors of cardstock. Attach to layout, layering as desired.

3 Apply felt sticker to cardstock circle and write journaling on tag. Affix both to layout. Add letter stickers for title and finish with pen. Machine-stitch as desired. Complete with brads.

TOTAL TIME TO SCRAPLIFT:

## 45
minutes

☐ 2 sheets cardstock

☐ 2 sheets patterned paper
(striped and flocked)

☐ 2 sets letter stickers

☐ 2 border stickers
(dot and flourish)

☐ 1 yard rickrack

☐ 1 pen

☐ 6 photographs

### just add

☐ 1 paper border (flowers)

**Ice Cream Social** by Suzy Plantamura. **Supplies** *Cardstock:* Bazzill Basics Paper; *Patterned paper:* BasicGrey (pink) and Doodlebug Design (white flocked); *Chipboard letter stickers:* Heidi Swapp for Advantus; *Letter stickers and paper border:* Doodlebug Design; *Border stickers:* KI Memories; *Border punch:* Fiskars; *Pen:* Sakura; *Other:* Rickrack.

## make it
(even) easier!

Substitute lace or
premade borders for the
punched paper edge.

every year the school has an ice cream social where all the kids dress in fifties attire. Chloe had so much fun dancing with Nicole!

## INSTRUCTIONS

**1** Use border punch to scallop edge of flocked paper. Attach to pink cardstock. Line up six photos across middle of layout. (Note: Suzy left one photo larger for variety.)

**2** Add paper border, patterned-paper strips and border stickers along top and bottom of photos.

**3** Draw wavy lines and write journaling. Finish with letter stickers for title.

TOTAL TIME TO SCRAPLIFT:

## 45
### minutes

## from the pantry

☐ 2 sheets cardstock

☐ 1 sheet patterned paper (cartoon)

☐ 2 chipboard stars

☐ 1 star sticker

☐ 2 sets letter stickers

☐ 2 pens (black and white)

☐ 1 computer font

☐ 4 photographs  4×6

## just add

☐ Chalk

**The Superhero and the Cheerleader** by Lisa Dickinson. **Supplies** *Cardstock:* Bazzill Basics Paper; *Patterned paper:* Prima; *Letter stickers:* Imagination Project; *Chipboard stars and letters:* Heidi Swapp for Advantus; *Yellow stickers:* KI Memories; *Chalk:* Craft-T Products; *Font:* You Are Loved; *Other:* Pens.

## make it (even) easier!

Skip the coloring and leave the paper black and white.

## INSTRUCTIONS

1 Cut top one-third of patterned paper off and attach both pieces to cardstock as shown. (If desired, color portions of the design.) Mat photos and attach to layout.

2 Create large title word and journaling on computer, cut out and glue to page.

3 Embellish with chipboard and sticker stars. Finish title with stickers and pen.

TOTAL TIME TO SCRAPLIFT:

## 30 minutes

### from the pantry

- ☐ 4 sheets cardstock
- ☐ 2 sheets patterned paper (striped and number)
- ☐ 1 set letter stickers
- ☐ 1 felt sticker accent
- ☐ 2 computer fonts
- ☐ 7 photographs

### just add

- ☐ 1 paper border (scallop)

## make it (even) easier!

Add additional photos in place of the patterned paper in the center of the layout.

**Dinner Alaskan Style** by Courtney Kelly. **Supplies** *Cardstock:* Bazzill Basics Paper; *Patterned paper:* Sassafras; *Letter stickers:* Making Memories; *Felt fish:* Fancy Pants Designs; *Paper border:* Doodlebug Design; *Fonts:* AL Highlight and King; *Other:* Corner-rounder punch.

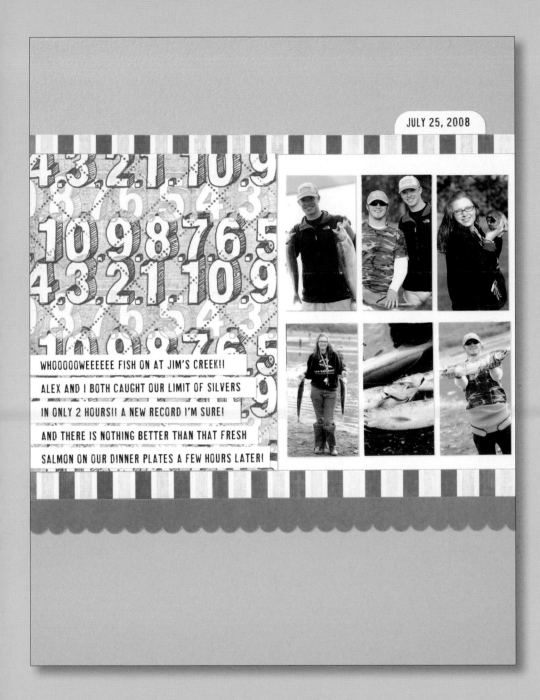

JULY 25, 2008

WHOOOOOWEEEEEE FISH ON AT JIM'S CREEK!!

ALEX AND I BOTH CAUGHT OUR LIMIT OF SILVERS

IN ONLY 2 HOURS!! A NEW RECORD I'M SURE!

AND THERE IS NOTHING BETTER THAN THAT FRESH

SALMON ON OUR DINNER PLATES A FEW HOURS LATER!

## INSTRUCTIONS

**1** Cut section of white cardstock and place it as shown, above vertical center of blue cardstock background. Edge top of section with strip of striped paper and bottom with striped paper and scallop paper border. Add a block of patterned paper to inside of right-hand page.

**2** Trim six photos to approximately 1" x 2" and mat them in a grid on white portion of right-hand page. Place large photo on left-hand page.

**3** Type journaling on computer, cut into strips and affix to layout. Round corners of date strip and attach. Complete by adding title, using embellishment to replace one of the letters.

# 30
minutes

## from the pantry

- ☐ 5 sheets cardstock (1 laser-cut)
- ☐ 1 sheet patterned paper (striped)
- ☐ 1 set letter stickers
- ☐ 1 sticker accent
- ☐ 2 rhinestone brads
- ☐ 1 computer font
- ☐ 4 photographs

## just add

- ☐ 1 tree die cut

**The Perfect Tree** by Dawn Carlisle. **Photos** by Hannah Carlisle. **Supplies** *Cardstock:* Bazzill Basics Paper (red), Die Cuts With a View (green) and The Paper Company (white); *Patterned paper:* Chatterbox; *Red foil stickers and rhinestone brads:* Making Memories; *Digital cutter:* Xyron Wishblade; *Border punch:* Fiskars; *Font:* VAG Rounded BT; *Other:* Dingbat tree font.

## make it (even) easier!

Don't have a digital cutter? Letter stickers and a die cut can create the same effect.

December 7, 2007

It was a beautiful day for hunting for our Christmas Tree. The sun was shining but the weather was crisp... absolutely perfect weather for choosing our tree. Dad & Hannah picked a very large Douglas Fir.

## INSTRUCTIONS

1 Mat photos on white cardstock, leaving equal margins between them. Print journaling and mat on blue cardstock. Attach journaling box to layout to complete grid. Affix all to red cardstock background.

2 Add strips of striped paper to top and bottom of photo grid. Punch border strips and attach.

3 Create title and tree accent with digital cutter. Finish with stickers and brads.

TOTAL TIME TO SCRAPLIFT:

# 45
minutes

## from the pantry

☐ 4 sheets cardstock

☐ 3 sheets patterned paper
(striped, diamond and word)

☐ 3 sets letter stickers

☐ 4 word stickers

☐ 1 journaling stamp

☐ 1 inkpad

☐ Embroidery floss

☐ 1 pen

☐ 4 photographs

## just add

☐ 1 metal clip

## make it
(even) easier!

Instead of an enlargement,
substitute another 4" x 6" picture
for the focal-point photo.

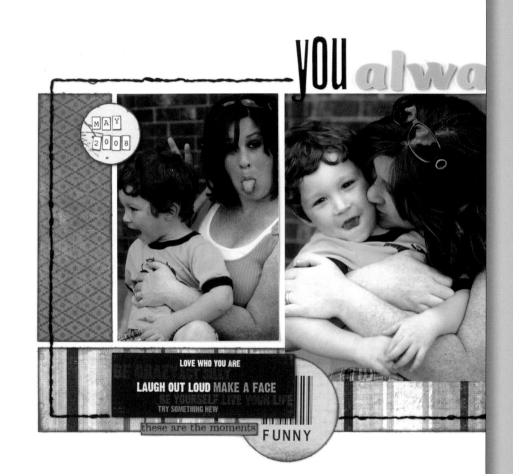

**You Always Make Me Smile** by Allison Davis. **Supplies** *Cardstock:* Bazzill Basics Paper; *Patterned paper and die cuts:* My Mind's Eye; *Letter stickers:* American Crafts ("Always" and "Smile"), EK Success ("May 2008") and Rusty Pickle ("You" and "Make Me"); *Word stickers:* EK Success; *Metal clip:* Making Memories; *Journaling stamp:* Autumn Leaves; *Ink:* ColorBox, Clearsnap; *Embroidery floss:* DMC; *Pen:* Zig Writer, EK Success.

## INSTRUCTIONS

1   Ink strip of striped paper and attach near bottom edge of layout. Position four vertical photos above the striped paper, letting the 5" x 7" photo overlap.

2   Add blocks of inked patterned paper to the right and left of photos. Stitch around outside of design, along inner edge of patterned papers and just above photographs.

3   Add title letters and various embellishments. Handwrite journaling.

## from the pantry

- ☐ 3 sheets patterned paper (striped, leaf and grid)
- ☐ 1 set rub-on words
- ☐ 1 sheet rub-on dotted lines
- ☐ 3 chipboard accents
- ☐ Thread
- ☐ 1 pen
- ☐ 1 computer font
- ☐ 3 photographs

## just add

- ☐ 1 set chipboard letters

### INSTRUCTIONS

1. Use a plate to trace circle out of patterned paper. Attach to grid background paper. Place strip of striped paper vertically down center of circle and stitch to adhere.

2. Place photos along striped strip, overlapping slightly. Add title and chipboard accents. Write date.

3. Create journaling on computer, print and cut into strips, and attach to layout. Finish with rub-on words and dots to frame edges.

**Create** by Kim Arnold. **Supplies** *Patterned paper, chipboard letters and accents:* Scenic Route; *Rub-ons:* KI Memories (dots) and Scenic Route (words); *Font:* Arial; *Other:* Thread and pen.

## make it (even) easier!

Hand-draw the lines or use rub-ons to replicate the look of stitching.

TOTAL TIME TO SCRAPLIFT:

20
minutes

**Carousel** by Nicole Samuels. **Supplies** *Cardstock:* Bazzill Basics Paper; *Patterned paper and chipboard letter stickers:* American Crafts; *Mini letter stickers:* Making Memories; *Tickets:* Creative Café, Creative Imaginations; *Pen:* American Crafts.

## from the pantry

- ☐ 1 sheet cardstock
- ☐ 2 sheets patterned paper (swirl and floral)
- ☐ 2 sets letter stickers (1 mini)
- ☐ 1 pen
- ☐ 3 photographs

## just add

- ☐ 3 ticket die cuts

## make it (even) easier!

Use ribbon to border the bottom of the photos.

## INSTRUCTIONS

1 Cut designs from a large patterned paper and adhere to cardstock background. Attach three vertical photos in white space.

2 Apply title letters along edge of paper. Use cutout designs from patterned paper as border for bottom of photos and as replacement for one title letter.

3 Add tickets and journaling.

TOTAL TIME TO SCRAPLIFT:

# 1
## hour

## from the pantry

☐  5 sheets cardstock

☐  3 sheets patterned paper
(striped and starburst)

☐  2 sets letter stickers

☐  3 stamps (notebook paper,
sun and circle)

☐  3 inkpads

☐  2 ribbon scraps

☐  2 pens

☐  4 photographs

## just add

☐  Rhinestones

**Splash Time** by Angie Hagist. **Supplies** *Cardstock:* Bazzill Basics Paper (red, orange and teal) and Prism Papers (white); *Patterned paper:* KI Memories (striped) and We R Memory Keepers (orange crackle); *Stamps:* Inque Boutique; *Ink:* Close To My Heart; *Letter stickers:* Doodlebug Design ("Splash") and Karen Foster Design ("Time"); *Ribbon:* May Arts; *Rhinestones:* Jo-Ann Stores; *Corner-rounder punch:* McGill; *Pens:* Sharpie, Newell Rubbermaid (green) and Sakura (black).

## make it
## (even) easier!

Use notepad paper in place of
the notepad stamp.

## INSTRUCTIONS

**1** Attach red cardstock to patterned-paper background, rounding left corners. Place photos in a block. Add thin strip of striped paper along bottom of photos.

**2** Stamp sun images (for letter background), circle image (for accent) and notepad-paper images (for journaling) and cut out. Handwrite journaling. Cut slits in paper and attach journaling to layout with ribbons.

**3** Mount letters on stamped sun circles and affix to layout. Add letter stickers and other embellishments. Add dots around edge of arrow. Accent background paper with rhinestones.

## 20 minutes

### from the pantry

☐  3 sheets cardstock

☐  1 sheet patterned paper (shaped)

☐  1 set rub-on letters

☐  2 epoxy stickers

☐  1 pen

☐  7 photographs

### just add

☐  1 acrylic accent

**dream**

**field trip**

*This has to be one of my favorite field trips ever! Krispy Kreme doughnuts on an early fall morning - who wouldn't want to sign up to chaperone this one?! Elizabeth was in 3/4s at Stanley Clark - Mrs. Matthys and Mrs. Stahl were her teachers that year. The children all got hats to wear (+ so did I) and were allowed to watch the doughnuts being made through the glass. But, not only that! They were brought back into the kitchen and got to see the dough being made and talk to the employees. Pretty big stuff for 3-4 year olds! But, of course, the best part was the free doughnuts at the end of the tour. Elizabeth chose sprinkles - of course - and declared it to be delicious. Her little group of friends that day included Emily, Francie and Grace and they were simply too cute for words! (04/05)*

**Field Trip** by Stephanie Vetne. **Supplies** *Cardstock:* Bazzill Basics Paper; *Patterned paper:* Making Memories; *Epoxy sticker:* Autumn Leaves; *Acrylic accent:* KI Memories; *Rub-on letters:* Doodlebug Design; *Pen:* Creative Memories.

## make it (even) easier!

Draw teal lines on the right side with a marker instead of cutting paper strips.

## INSTRUCTIONS

1 Leaving 1" at top and bottom, create photo block on right side of layout. Add strips of teal paper to top and bottom edges.

2 Adhere patterned paper so it goes off right edge of left side of layout. Attach photos, continuing the line from right side. Handwrite journaling on patterned paper.

3 Apply rub-ons for title and accent with embellishments.

TOTAL TIME TO SCRAPLIFT:

## 45
minutes

### from the pantry

☐ 2 sheets cardstock

☐ 4 sheets patterned paper
(green, starburst and 2 dot)

☐ 2 sets letter stickers

☐ 3 sticker accents

☐ 1 inkpad

☐ Embroidery floss

☐ 1 pen

☐ 5 photographs

### just add

☐ 3 transparencies

## make it
(even) easier!

No transparencies?
Substitute photos or
patterned-paper blocks.

On a warm Sunday in July we went to what used to be Exotic Animal Paradise. I now know why they dropped the "Exotic" part. We saw deer, something we named a zonkey because it looked like a donkey with zebra stripes, some cows and a smelly camel that Drew was brave enough to feed. The only thing that made the day fun was seeing how much Drew enjoyed it.

**Animal Paradise** by Allison Davis. **Supplies** *Cardstock:* Bazzill Basics Paper; *Patterned paper:* Scenic Route; *Letter stickers:* Doodlebug Design and Pebbles Inc.; *Transparencies:* Hambly Screen Prints; *Ink:* ColorBox, Clearsnap; *Embroidery floss:* DMC; *Pen:* Sakura; *Other:* Thread and sticker accents.

## INSTRUCTIONS

1  Cut four strips of patterned paper. Ink and attach to cardstock background.

2  Position photographs and adhere, filling empty spots with animal-print transparency blocks. Stitch around perimeter of photos.

3  Add title letters and stickers, and handwrite journaling.

## 40
## minutes

## from the pantry

☐ 3 sheets of cardstock

☐ 1 sheet of rub-on letters

☐ 2 computer fonts

☐ 6 photographs

## just add

☐ 1 rub-on date

On the way home from Ohio we stopped at Wisconsin Dells. Since we were only there one night we skipped the water parks, knowing we'd never get you kids to leave. Sorry guys, we'll have to go back when you're older! But we did go on the famous Duck ride before we took off back home to Minnesota. It was such an enjoyable ride and our tour guide was a hoot. We got lucky and saw some deer before our tour was over. And of course before we left town, we managed to bring home a certain turtle, but that of course is another story!

**The Wisconsin Dells** by Rhonda Stark
**Supplies** *Software:* Adobe Photoshop, Adobe Systems; *Digital paper:* Gina Cabrera, *www.digitaldesignessentials.com*; *Computer fonts:* AL Cleanliness, "15 Handwritten Fonts" CD and AL Modern Type, "15 Typewriter Fonts" CD, Autumn Leaves.

## INSTRUCTIONS

1 Print your journaling on a sheet of kraft-colored cardstock.

2 Trim a block of white cardstock and a strip of black cardstock and adhere them to the background.

3 Crop your photos and arrange them on the page. Apply rub-on letters to a strip of cardstock to create the title, then adhere it to the page. Add the rub-on date.

# GingERBREaD 101

**Gingerbread 101** by Rachel Ludwig
**Supplies** *Textured cardstock:* Bazzill Basics Paper; *Patterned paper and letter stickers:* BasicGrey; *Felt numbers:* Kunin Felt; *Letter stamps:* Fontwerks; *Stamping ink:* ColorBox, Clearsnap; *Other:* Brads.

TOTAL TIME TO SCRAPLIFT:

## 30 minutes

### from the pantry

- ☐ 1 sheet of cardstock
- ☐ 6 strips of patterned paper (textured)
- ☐ 1 sheet of letter stickers
- ☐ 1 set of letter stamps
- ☐ 1 inkpad
- ☐ 6 brads
- ☐ 1 square punch (optional)
- ☐ 6 photographs

### just add

- ☐ 1 package of felt numbers

## make it (even) easier!

Handwrite your journaling strips, and use number stickers instead of felt numbers.

## INSTRUCTIONS

1 Crop or punch your photos into squares and adhere them to the page.

2 Add letter stickers and felt numbers to create the title.

3 Stamp your journaling on patterned-paper strips and attach them to the layout with brads.

TOTAL TIME TO SCRAPLIFT:

# 20 minutes

## make it (even) easier!

Create a border using
ribbon, a strip of patterned
paper, a row of brads
or a border sticker instead
of ephemera.

**Packing** by Lisa Brown Caveney
**Supplies** *Patterned paper:* 7gypsies; *Letter stickers:* American Crafts;
*Pen:* Zig Writer, EK Success.

## INSTRUCTIONS

1 Create the background with patterned paper, adding a strip of white cardstock to the left side of the layout. Place the memorabilia (packing stickers) to cover the edges.

2 Arrange two horizontal 4" x 6" photos and three vertical 4" x 6" photos on the patterned paper to form a large photo block.

3 Complete the layout by adding a title with letter stickers and handwriting your journaling (vertically) on the white strip.

## 30 minutes

### from the pantry

- ☐ 4 sheets of cardstock
- ☐ 1 pen
- ☐ 3 pieces of ribbon
- ☐ 3 staples
- ☐ 5 photographs

### just add

- ☐ 1 sheet of word stickers

**E Is for Escape** by Heather Preckel
**Supplies** *Textured cardstock:* Bazzill Basics Paper; *Stickers:* 7gypsies; *Ribbon:* Michaels; *Staples:* Target; *Pen:* Zig Millennium, EK Success.

## make it (even) easier!

Replace the doodling with rub-on images or omit the doodling entirely.

## INSTRUCTIONS

1 Cut a 10" x 10" cardstock square and layer your photographs over it. Adhere it to a piece of 12" x 12" cardstock.

2 Handwrite your journaling underneath the photo block. For extra visual interest, use word stickers in your journaling. Add doodling to the page as desired.

3 Tie ribbon around a 2" x 12" strip of cardstock and adhere it to the background cardstock. Place a large sticker in the lower-right corner of the page.

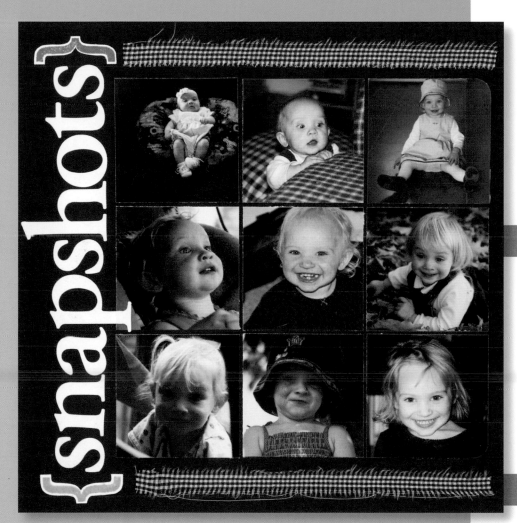

Snapshots by Heather Preckel
**Supplies** *Textured cardstock:* Bazzill Basics Paper; *Fabric:* Wal-Mart; *Bracket stamps:* Wendi Speciale Designs; *Letter stickers:* American Crafts; *Stamping ink:* Ranger Industries.

TOTAL TIME TO SCRAPLIFT:

## 30 minutes

## from the pantry

- ☐ 2 sheets of cardstock
- ☐ 1 sheet of letter stickers
- ☐ 1 punctuation stamp (from letter stamp set)
- ☐ 2 inkpads
- ☐ 9 photographs

## just add

- ☐ 2 strips of fabric

## INSTRUCTIONS

1 Crop nine photos into 3" x 3" squares and arrange them in a square on black cardstock.

2 Use letter stickers and stamps to create the title.

3 Fray some fabric strips and attach them along the top and bottom of the page.

## make it (even) easier!

Create the title on your computer and print it on cardstock.

Replace the brackets with another appropriate punctuation mark or dingbat included in your letter stamp set or on your sheet of letter stickers.

Use two strips of ribbon instead of fraying fabric strips.

TOTAL TIME TO SCRAPLIFT:

# 30
## minutes

☐ 3 sheets of cardstock

☐ 1 pen

☐ 1 sheet of rub-on letters

☐ 6 photographs **4×6**

## just add

☐ 1 printed map

**Cross Country** by Lisa Brown Caveney
**Supplies** *Rub-on letters:* Making Memories; *Pen:* Zig Writer, EK Success; *Other:* Printed map.

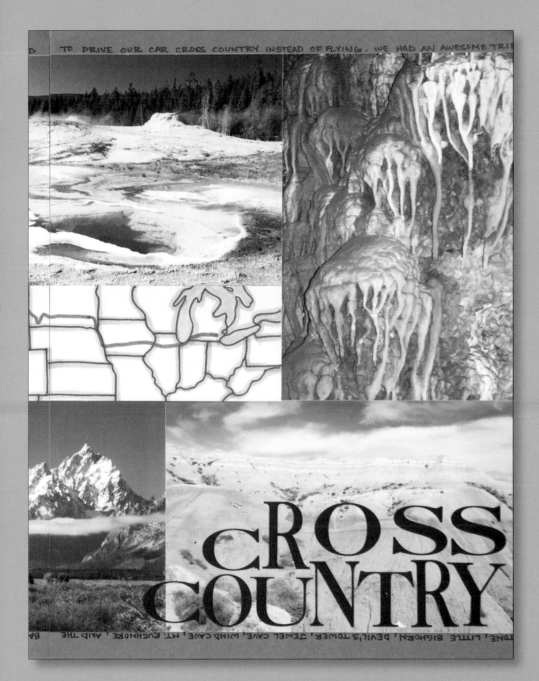

## INSTRUCTIONS

1. Arrange six 4" x 6" photos (two vertical, four horizontal) around the outside edges of the layout.

2. Scan a map (or find an image online) and print it on a 2" x 8" strip of white cardstock. Attach the map to the center of the layout.

3. Use rub-on letters to create the title, and handwrite your journaling around the outside edges of the layout.

TOTAL TIME TO SCRAPLIFT:

## 20 minutes

### from the pantry

☐ 3 sheets of cardstock

☐ 5 scraps of patterned paper cut into very thin strips (assorted)

☐ 1 computer font

☐ 3 photographs

### just add

☐ 8 buttons

## make it (even) easier!

Use two strips of patterned paper instead of multiple thin strips.

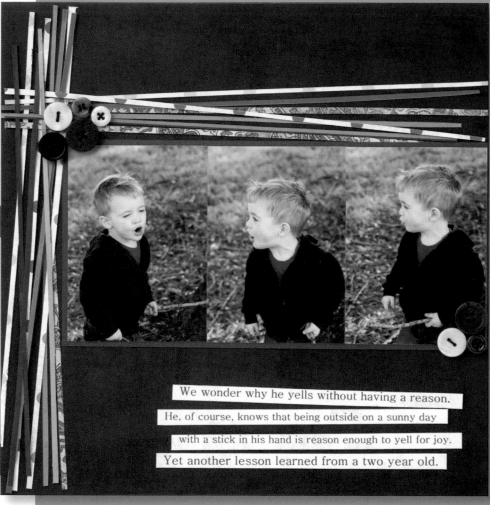

We wonder why he yells without having a reason. He, of course, knows that being outside on a sunny day with a stick in his hand is reason enough to yell for joy. Yet another lesson learned from a two year old.

**Yell** by April Peterson
**Supplies** *Textured cardstock:* Bazzill Basics Paper; *Patterned papers:* KI Memories and My Mind's Eye; *Computer font:* Batang, downloaded from the Internet; *Other:* Buttons.

## INSTRUCTIONS

1 Line up three 3½" x 5" photos and mount them on a sheet of cardstock. Trim the excess and attach the photo block to a sheet of cardstock

2 Cut the patterned paper into thin strips and attach them to the page.

3 Trim the printed journaling strips and adhere them to the page. Accent the page with buttons.

## bonus project

Don't let your project scraps go to waste! April created this darling card from the leftover scraps from her layout.

**Thinking of You Card (from "Yell" scraps)** by April Peterson
**Supplies** *Textured cardstock:* Bazzill Basics Paper; *Patterned papers:* KI Memories and My Mind's Eye; *Tag:* Making Memories; *Other:* Buttons and thread.

## 30 minutes

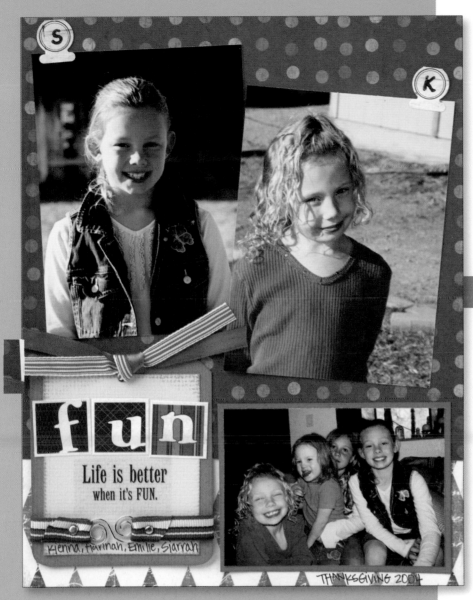

**Fun** by Dece Gherardini
**Supplies** *Textured cardstock and stamping ink:* Bazzill Basics Paper; *Patterned paper and letter stickers:* Scenic Route Paper Co.; *Quote sticker:* Wordsworth; *Ribbon:* May Arts; *Tabs:* 7gypsies; *Spiral clip:* Making Memories; *Pen:* Pigma Micron, Sakura.

## from the pantry

- ☐ 3 strips of cardstock
- ☐ 2 pieces of patterned paper (geometric)
- ☐ 1 sheet of letter stickers
- ☐ 3 pieces of ribbon
- ☐ 2 brads
- ☐ 1 paper clip
- ☐ 1 pen
- ☐ 1 sticker
- ☐ 1 inkpad
- ☐ 1 set of letter stamps
- ☐ 3 photographs

## just add

- ☐ 2 letter tabs

## INSTRUCTIONS

1 Create the page background using two coordinating patterned papers.

2 Mat your focal-point photo and adhere all three photos to the page. Stamp a letter on each tab and adhere them to the top two photos.

3 Add your title and phrase stickers to a small piece of cardstock. Mat it and punch a hole in the top for ribbon. Wrap ribbon around the bottom and fasten it with a decorative paper clip and mini brads.

TOTAL TIME TO SCRAPLIFT:

## 30 minutes

### from the pantry

- ☐ 2 sheets of cardstock
- ☐ 8 strips of patterned paper (3 geometric, 2 textured, 3 striped)
- ☐ 3 sheets of letter stickers
- ☐ 1 pen
- ☐ 1 inkpad
- ☐ 3 photographs **4×6**

### just add

- ☐ 1 sheet of rub-on accents

## make it (even) easier!

Look for patterned papers that feature multiple strips of different designs on a single sheet of paper. They're an easy, inexpensive solution for mixing patterns.

**Sparkler Art** by Shannon Zickel
**Supplies** *Patterned papers:* American Crafts, Scenic Route Paper Co., Making Memories and K&Company; *Letter stickers:* American Crafts and Heidi Swapp for Advantus; *Rub-ons and decorative tape:* Heidi Swapp for Advantus; *Stamping ink:* Inkadinkado; *Pen:* Pigment Pro, American Crafts.

Kinda lame! but that was — so not the case! we enjoyed
night just being together. You went through sparkler
designs in the sky! Daddy couldn't light them fast
uncomplicated - No pushing - Fun Night! July 4th 2005.

## INSTRUCTIONS

1. Slightly crop your photos and arrange them on your layout.

2. Apply letter stickers along the left side of the layout and across the bottom of the right page to create your title.

3. Handwrite your journaling along the bottom of the layout. Embellish with small scraps of patterned paper and rub-on accents.

TOTAL TIME TO SCRAPLIFT:

## 30 minutes

### from the pantry

☐ 2 sheets of cardstock

☐ 2 sheets of patterned paper (textured)

☐ 2 sheets of rub-on letters

☐ 1 pen

☐ 7 photographs

### just add

☐ 2 tickets as page accents

**Fair Rides** by Rhonda Stark
**Supplies** *Software:* Adobe Photoshop, Adobe Systems; *Digital kraft paper:* Gina Cabrera, *www.digitaldesignessentials.com; Digital white-and-blue paper:* Katie Pertiet, *www.designerdigitals.com; Digital fair tickets (re-colored):* Holly Craig, source unknown; *Computer fonts:* Susie's Hand and Shortcut, downloaded from the Internet.

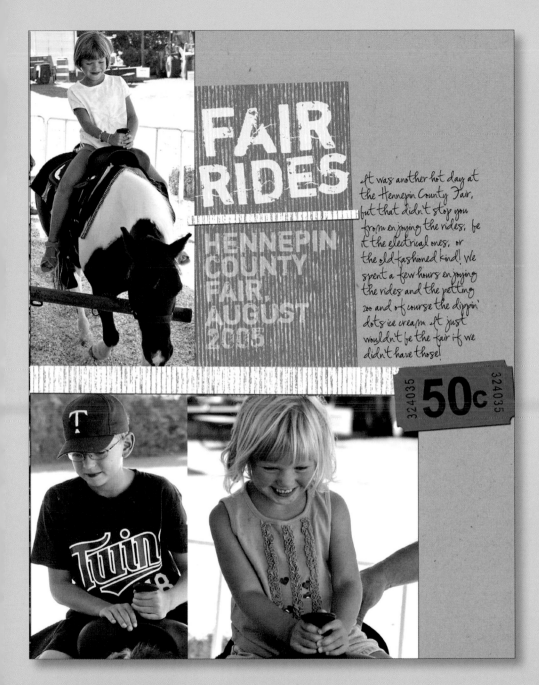

FAIR RIDES

HENNEPIN COUNTY FAIR AUGUST 2005

It was another hot day at the Hennepin County Fair, but that didn't stop you from enjoying the rides, be it the electrical ones, or the old fashioned kind! We spent a few hours enjoying the rides and the petting zoo and of course the dippin' dots ice cream. It just wouldn't be the fair if we didn't have those!

50c  324035  324035

INSTRUCTIONS

1 Adhere a block of patterned paper to each page of the background.

2 Crop your photos to fit and arrange them on the layout. Place strips of textured patterned paper horizontally, where the photos meet.

3 Apply rub-ons to create your title, and handwrite your journaling.

TOTAL TIME TO SCRAPLIFT:

# 30
## minutes

## from the pantry

☐ 2 sheets of cardstock

☐ 10 staples

☐ 1 pen

☐ 1 set of letter/number stamps

☐ 1 inkpad

☐ 5 photographs

## just add

☐ 1 graphic rub-on

## make it (even) easier!

Instead of using a rub-on image as a page accent, use a sticker or a rubber stamp.

**Goodbye** by Rhonda Stark
**Supplies** *Software:* Adobe Photoshop, Adobe Systems; *Digital papers, stamps and staples:* Gina Cabrera, *www.digitaldesignessentials.com; Digital lines:* Katie Pertiet, *www.designerdigitals.com;* *Computer font:* TIA A Capital Idea, Tia Bennett, *www.designerdigitals.com.*

## INSTRUCTIONS

1 Crop your photos and cardstock into 2" x 2" squares. Attach them to the background cardstock with staples.

2 Stamp numbers on journaling squares and stamp your title.

3 Handwrite your journaling over the stamped numbers and add a handwritten subtitle over the title. For a decorative effect, draw a square around the layout.

TOTAL TIME TO SCRAPLIFT:

## 30 minutes

*Your very first taste of a old American favorite! You weren't quite sure of what to think at first - but after a few bites you liked it!*

Cotton Candy

**Cotton Candy** by Heather Preckel
**Supplies** *Textured cardstock:* Bazzill Basics Paper; *Patterned papers and monogram:* BasicGrey; *Rub-on letters:* Scrapworks; *Pen:* Pigment Pro, American Crafts; *Other:* Ribbon.

## from the pantry

- ☐ 1 sheet of cardstock
- ☐ 3 sheets of patterned paper (1 geometric, 1 striped, 1 textured)
- ☐ 1 pen
- ☐ 1 sheet of rub-on letters
- ☐ 1 piece of ribbon
- ☐ 4 photographs

## just add

- ☐ 1 monogram letter

## INSTRUCTIONS

1 Cut an 11" x 6" strip of patterned paper and adhere it to the background cardstock.

2 Mat your largest photo on patterned paper and adhere all the photos to the layout. (*Tip:* Use foam squares or adhesive dots if you want a dimensional effect.)

3 Tie a piece of ribbon to your monogram accent and then adhere the monogram to the page as the first letter of your title. Finish your title with rub-on letters. Handwrite your journaling.

## make it (even) easier!

Omit the monogram letter and create the title entirely with rub-on letters, stamps or stickers.

TOTAL TIME TO SCRAPLIFT:

## 1 hour

- ☐ 2 sheets of cardstock
- ☐ 4 sheets of patterned paper (2 floral, 2 textured)
- ☐ 1 sheet of letter stickers
- ☐ 1 pen
- ☐ 1 set of letter stamps
- ☐ 1 inkpad
- ☐ 1 computer font
- ☐ 12 photographs

## just add

- ☐ 2 paper flowers

**Luau Party** by Tracey Odachowski
**Supplies** *Textured cardstock:* Bazzill Basics Paper; *Patterned papers:* BasicGrey; *Letter stickers:* American Crafts; *Letter stamps:* Making Memories; *Stamping ink:* Stampin' Up!; *Pen:* Uni-ball Signo, Sanford; *Paper flowers:* Prima; *Computer fonts:* Arial, Microsoft Word; Sandpaper, downloaded from the Internet.

## make it (even) easier!

Use circles of patterned paper instead of paper flowers.

Use letter stickers instead of letter stamps for the title.

Use premade number accents instead of cutting out the large numbers.

## INSTRUCTIONS

1 Cut two sheets of floral patterned paper to 10" x 9" and attach them to the background. Cut the textured patterned papers to 9¾" x 8½" and mount them over the floral patterned paper.

2 Crop and adhere your photos. Create the title blocks using scraps of floral patterned paper.

3 Print two large numbers (or letters) on scraps of textured patterned paper and cut and adhere them to the page. Stamp your title and then embellish the layout with letter stamps, letter stickers, paper flowers and journaling.

# 45
## minutes

## from the pantry

- ☐ 2 sheets of cardstock

- ☐ 6 thin strips of patterned paper (2 geometric, 2 striped, 2 text)

- ☐ 1 block of patterned paper (striped)

- ☐ 2 sheets or various patterned-paper scraps for punching out elements (1 striped, 1 geometric)

- ☐ 1 sheet of rub-on letters

- ☐ 1 computer font

- ☐ 1 small square punch

- ☐ 9 photographs

## just add

- ☐ 1 word sticker

**Field Trip** by Annie Weis
**Supplies** *Textured cardstock:* Bazzill Basics Paper; *Patterned papers:* KI Memories and Scenic Route Paper Co.; *Rub-on letters:* Scenic Route Paper Co.; *Word sticker:* 7gypsies; *Computer font:* Futura Book BT, downloaded from the Internet.

## make it (even) easier!

Handwrite your journaling.

Use letter stickers for your title.

Instead of affixing punched-out squares of patterned paper
in a row, just use another strip of patterned paper.

## INSTRUCTIONS

1 Arrange your 3" x 5" photos edge to edge in the middle of a 12" x 12" sheet of cardstock.

2 Trim your printed journaling to a 3" x 5" rectangle, leaving room to add rub-on letters for the title. Punch squares from patterned paper with colors that coordinate with your layout.

3 Adhere punched-out squares and thin strips of patterned paper to accent the layout. Place a word sticker in the upper-left corner of the layout.

TOTAL TIME TO SCRAPLIFT:

## 20
minutes

## from the pantry

☐ 3 sheets of cardstock

☐ 1 sheet of patterned paper
(striped)

☐ 2 computer fonts

☐ 1 inkpad

☐ 5 photographs **4×6**

## plus one

☐ 1 pair of decorative-edged
scissors

### INSTRUCTIONS

1 Cut a 12" x 12" piece of patterned paper into two 12" x 6" pieces and adhere them to the cardstock background.

2 Line up four pictures across the two pages. Mount your focal-point photo on cardstock and place it in the lower-left corner of the layout.

3 Add strips of cardstock cut with decorative-edged scissors above and below the row of photos. Ink the edges of the printed journaling block and adhere it to the layout.

**I'm Gonna Get You!** by April Peterson
**Supplies** *Textured cardstock:* Bazzill Basics
Paper; *Patterned paper:* Chatterbox;
*Stamping ink:* ColorBox, Clearsnap;
*Computer fonts:* Century Gothic and
Times New Roman, Microsoft Word;
*Other:* Decorative-edged scissors

These are the words that send you running and squealing every single time
we say them. "*I'm gonna get you!*" and you run. We don't even have
to actually try to 'get you' the words alone are enough.

These words are a valuable part of our day. They are cure for any grumpy
mood; perfect for expending that last bit of energy before bedtime, or for
ushering you back home (without you realizing it) at the end of a walk.

"*I'm gonna get you!*"

And when you are tired of the game, you come up to me, pull me down to
your level and give me a kiss. Thus, 'getting me' every time.

## make it (even) easier!

Instead of using
decorative-edged scissors,
use a straight-edge trimmer,
or use ribbon instead.

## bonus project

Don't let your project scraps go to waste! April
created this darling card from the leftover scraps
from her layout.

**Thank-You Card (from "I'm Gonna Get You!" scraps)** by April Peterson
**Supplies** *Textured cardstock and brads:* Bazzill Basics Paper; *Patterned
paper:* Chatterbox; *Rub-on:* Karen Foster Design; *Chipboard bookplate:*
Heidi Swapp for Advantus.

TOTAL TIME TO SCRAPLIFT:

## 45
minutes

☐ 2 sheets of cardstock

☐ 1 strip of patterned paper
(numbers or text)

☐ 2 sheets of letter stickers

☐ 1 package of brads

☐ 1 pen

☐ 2 pieces of ribbon

☐ 5 photographs  4×6

## just add

☐ 1 sheet of printed vellum

**Dollar Dance** by Melanie Bauer
**Supplies** *Textured cardstock:* Bazzill Basics Paper; *Patterned paper:* 7gypsies;
*Vellum, ribbon and mailbox letters:* Flair Designs; *Letter stickers and pen:*
American Crafts; *Brads:* Boxer Scrapbook Productions.

over $200. that's how much cash andrea and nick raked in during a single song at their wedding reception. bills were extracted from wallets and lines were formed for both the bride and groom. people handed over their single dollar — or more! — and got their few seconds in the spotlight with either member of the bridal party. such a crazy tradition!

**Rdance**

## make it (even) easier!

Instead of brads, use a graphic stamp or draw an arrow to lead the viewer's eye to an element in the photos.

Use a large monogram or sticker that coordinates with the patterned paper and colors of the layout instead of cutting a custom accent (here, a dollar sign).

## INSTRUCTIONS

1 Adhere the title to the layout using two different styles of letter stickers. Handwrite your journaling next to the title.

2 Line up your photos underneath the title. Add ribbon beneath the photos. For visual effect, punctuate the space after the ribbon with a symbol cut from printed vellum.

3 Embellish the left page with patterned paper and brads.

TOTAL TIME TO SCRAPLIFT:

## 30
minutes

- ☐ 4 sheets of cardstock
- ☐ 1 computer font
- ☐ 1 sheet of letter stickers
- ☐ 1 set of letter stamps
- ☐ 1 inkpad
- ☐ 5 pieces of ribbon
- ☐ 1 small circle punch
  (or hole punch)
- ☐ 5 photographs

### just add

- ☐ 2 buttons

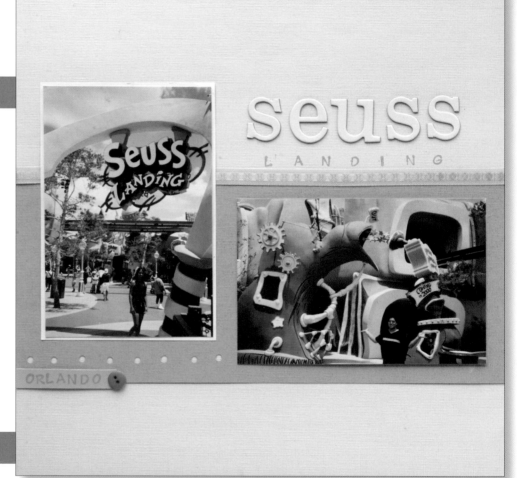

**Seuss Landing** by Nely Fok
**Supplies** *Textured cardstock:* Bazzill Basics Paper; *Chipboard letters:* Heidi Swapp for Advantus; *Letter stamps:* Hero Arts; *Stamping ink:* Ranger Industries; *Ribbon:* C.M. Offray & Son; *Other:* Buttons.

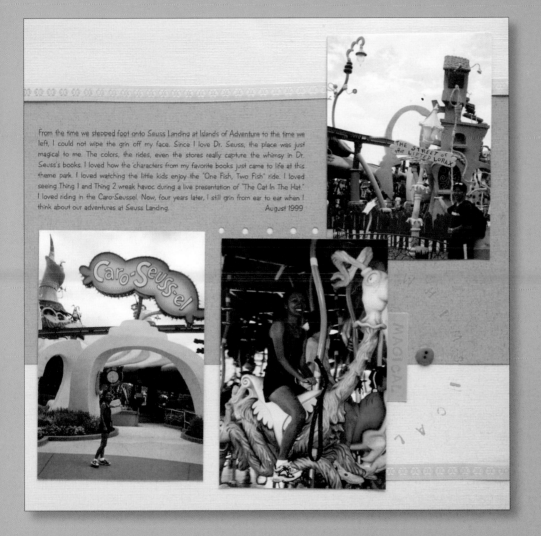

From the time we stepped foot onto Seuss Landing at Islands of Adventure to the time we left, I could not wipe the grin off my face. Since I love Dr. Seuss, the place was just magical to me. The colors, the rides, even the stores really capture the whimsy in Dr. Seuss's books. I loved how the characters from my favorite books just came to life at this theme park. I loved watching the little kids enjoy the "One Fish, Two Fish" ride. I loved seeing Thing 1 and Thing 2 wreak havoc during a live presentation of "The Cat In The Hat." I loved riding in the Caro-Seussel. Now, four years later, I still grin from ear to ear when I think about our adventures at Seuss Landing.                         August 1999

## INSTRUCTIONS

1 Print your journaling on a sheet of cardstock. Trim it and use it to color-block the page background.

2 Mat your focal-point photo and adhere all of the photos to the layout.

3 Combine letter stickers and stamps to create the title. Embellish the page with ribbon, rows of punched holes and buttons.

TOTAL TIME TO SCRAPLIFT:

## 30 minutes

## from the pantry

☐ 3 sheets of cardstock

☐ 2 strips of patterned paper (striped)

☐ 1 computer font

☐ 1 inkpad

☐ 2 circle punches (1 large, 1 small)

☐ 4 photographs 4×6

## just add

☐ 2 phrase stickers

**You Are So Silly** by April Peterson
**Supplies** *Textured cardstock:* Bazzill Basics Paper; *Patterned paper:* Kaleidoscope, My Mind's Eye; *Phrase stickers:* Carolee's Creations; *Circle punches:* EK Success; *Stamping ink:* ColorBox, Clearsnap; *Computer font:* 2Peas Weathered Fence, downloaded from www.twopeasinabucket.com.

## INSTRUCTIONS

1 Group four photos together on a sheet of cardstock. Cut two strips of patterned paper, ink the edges and use them to border the top and bottom of the photo block.

2 Mat the printed journaling and attach it to the layout.

3 Punch two circles and layer them. Apply a phrase sticker to the circle and to the top-left photo.

## bonus project

Don't let your project scraps go to waste! April created this darling card from the leftover scraps from her layout.

**Let the Good Times Roll Card (from "You Are So Silly" scraps)** by April Peterson
**Supplies** *Textured cardstock:* Bazzill Basics Paper; *Patterned paper:* Kaleidoscope, My Mind's Eye; *Sticker:* Carolee's Creations; *Stamping ink:* ColorBox, Clearsnap.

# 10 more easy techniques

Create cool accents and embellishments using just the basics—and maybe an extra supply here and there. Give these 10 great ideas a try:

1  Give your title extra punch by adhering your letter stickers directly over a portion of a photo. Try this with rub-on letters, too!
—Lisa Brown Caveney, Page 94

2  Emphasize your title by layering rub-on images over your letter stickers.
—Shannon Zickel, page 202

3 Call attention to a detail in a photo by creating a circle of brads around it.
—Shannon Zickel, page 102

4 Use your circle cutter to create large rings from patterned paper. Place them over the subjects of your photos to highlight them.
—Miriam Campbell, page 272

5  Stamp your journaling on strips of patterned paper. Use brads to attach the strips to your layout.
—Rachel Ludwig, page 193

6  Doodle your own page embellishments for a sweet, whimsical look. Vary the pen thickness for extra visual interest.
—Heather Preckel, page 196

7  Even the smallest scraps can be put to good use. Gather long, thin strips of patterned paper and cardstock together to create a cool and colorful page border. For additional detail, weave intersecting strips together and embellish with buttons.
—April Peterson, page 200

8 Use a paper clip as a ribbon holder. Loop the ends of the ribbon through each end of the paper clip. Fasten the ribbon ends together using brads.
—Dece Gherardini, page 201

9 Punch scraps of various patterned papers into small squares. Line them up to fashion an energetic border.
—Annie Weis, page 210

10   Give a stamped word a capricious feel by forming a half-circle with the letters. Try this with letter stickers and rub-ons, too!
—Nely Fok, page 216

## 30 minutes

### from the pantry

- ☐ 1 sheet of cardstock
- ☐ 1 sheet of patterned paper (striped)
- ☐ 2 sets of letter stickers
- ☐ 1 computer font
- ☐ 4 brads
- ☐ 1 piece of ribbon
- ☐ 1 circle punch
- ☐ 1 photograph **4×6**

### just add

- ☐ 3 scraps of patterned vellum

## make it (even) easier!

Omit the vellum scraps from your project. Create your title from just one sheet of letter stickers.

**2nd Birthday** by Kate Teague
**Supplies** *Patterned papers, vellum and letter stickers:* American Crafts; *Ribbon:* May Arts; *Circle punch:* EK Success; *Computer font:* Times New Roman, Microsoft Word; *Other:* Brads.

### INSTRUCTIONS

1 Print your journaling block and adhere it to a piece of patterned paper.

2 Mat your photo and attach it next to the journaling block.

3 Add letters stickers, a vellum strip and punched circle accents to finish your page.

happy family

# It's about the ⟶ cake

TOTAL TIME TO SCRAPLIFT:

## 30 minutes

It's true! How very selfish of us right? Well that's not the whole story. The cake has always been my family's way of indulging in their creative side all the while showing how much they care about the birthday person. My Mom was the one who started it all. She always made me the cutest cakes. I can still remember that teddy bear cake from my fifth birthday. I was so in love with that cake. And the fact that Mom let me pick the design and then help make it made it even more special. I have now brought Mackenzie into this tradition. It makes me so happy to make something extra special just for her. The past few years Tim has also become quite the cake maker. He has made me some amazing birthday cakes. I love that he takes a whole afternoon to craft something just for me rather than heading to the store and buying something fancy. So yes, I guess it is all about the cakes!

## from the pantry

☐  2 sheets of cardstock

☐  1 strip of patterned paper (striped)

☐  1 sheet of letter stickers

☐  1 circle punch

☐  1 computer font

☐  6 photographs

## just add

☐  1 phrase sticker

**It's All About the Cake** by Kate Teague
**Supplies** *Textured cardstock:* Bazzill Basics Paper; *Patterned paper:* KI Memories; *"C" letter sticker:* Doodlebug Design; *"A" letter sticker:* Creative Imaginations; *"E" letter sticker:* American Crafts; *"K" letter sticker:* Source unknown; *"Happy Family" sticker:* Die Cuts With a View; *Circle punch:* Creative Imaginations; *Computer font:* Century Gothic, downloaded from the Internet.

## INSTRUCTIONS

1 Print your journaling and the first half of your title on cardstock, leaving a space for the last title word.

2 Trim your photos. Line up the large photos along the bottom of the page. Mat the small photos on a strip of patterned paper and attach it to the top of the page.

3 Spell out the last title word with stickers. Attach the hand-cut cardstock arrow and the punched cardstock circles to complete the page.

# the pantry + 2 or 3

Now let's get out the good china and try a few recipes that are just a little more gourmet. Never fear—these projects don't require a trained chef, just a few additional ingredients.

TOTAL TIME TO SCRAPLIFT:

## 20
minutes

## from the pantry

☐  2 sheets cardstock

☐  1 sheet patterned paper (dot)

☐  12 word stickers

☐  1 border sticker

☐  1 circle sticker

☐  1 stamp

☐  1 inkpad

☐  1 pen

☐  4 photographs  **4×6**

## just add

☐  2 tab die cuts

☐  1 sheet vellum

## make it
(even) easier!

Symmetrically apply identical
embellishments to the right and left
of the photo block to replace the
product collages.

**Play All Day** by Karla Dudley. **Supplies** *Patterned paper, word stickers, border sticker, tabs, stamp and circle sticker:* October Afternoon; *Vellum:* Making Memories; *Ink:* Stampin' Up!; *Pen:* Pigma Micron, Sakura; *Other:* Staples.

## INSTRUCTIONS

1 Place four horizontal photos in center of two-page cardstock background.

2 Arrange word stickers and patterned paper strips in lines to right and left of photo block. Stamp swirl beneath each, and staple tabs to edge of photos.

3 Mat circle sticker on vellum and attach to center of layout. Journal around perimeter of photo block.

## 30 minutes

## from the pantry

- ☐ 1 sheet cardstock
- ☐ 1 sheet patterned paper (starburst)
- ☐ 2 sets mini letter stickers
- ☐ 1 title stamp
- ☐ 1 inkpad
- ☐ 2 sticker accents (word circle and sentiment strip)
- ☐ 1 chipboard date tab
- ☐ 1 computer font
- ☐ 1 photograph

## just add

- ☐ 1 transparency
- ☐ Notebook paper

### make it (even) easier!

Copy your journaling from a previously written blog or diary entry.

---

DON'T DO IT GO AHEAD STOP NOW WAIT A MINUTE HURRY UP SLOW DOWN

Why do I feel like I have no patience with you lately? You are a toddler and half the time you have no idea what you are doing or why. You are experimenting with the world and that's your job. It's your job to see how long it can take you to climb up a flight of stairs, and it's your job to figure out how to open the sippy cup and dump the water all over your book. Why do I have such high expectations of a 19 month old? I feel like all I do these days is tell you what to do and then put you in a time out when you don't do it. I hate that. I love you more than anything in this world, and all I want is to be a good mother to you. I hate thinking of you looking at a scowling face all the time.

I am so tired and out of breath from the pregnancy right now which is only going to get worse. Then when your little sister finally arrives I will be more exhausted than ever. I need to find a way to deal with this now. I know I will be frustrated with you at times, but I hate being impatient. I want to be more kind to you, and give you hugs and kisses even when you're not being a perfect angel. I shouldn't expect you to be a perfect angel, anyway. I am going to try really hard, Audrey. I am going to take more deep breaths, more counts to ten, and more deep looks into your beautiful brown eyes to know that you are not purposely trying to annoy me. You are just doing your job.

today

challenges

MAY 08

I wasn't The MOM I waNt To BE

**Today I Wasn't the Mom I Want to Be** by Lisa Kisch. **Supplies** *Cardstock:* The Write Stock; *Patterned paper:* Scenic Route; *Sticker:* 7gypsies; *Acrylic accents:* Hambly Screen Prints; *Letter stickers:* Autumn Leaves (red) and Making Memories (black); *Date tab:* Martha Stewart Crafts; *Stamp:* Ali Edwards for Cocoa Daisy; *Ink:* Close To My Heart.

## INSTRUCTIONS

1 Journal on computer and print on lined paper. Tear edges and attach to layout. Add photo and patterned-paper strip to left of journaling. Attach sentiment strip to left edge of photo.

2 Stamp "Today" and attach transparency beneath it. Top with date tab.

3 Add letter stickers to complete title.

## make it (even) easier!

Replace the word and letter sticker with handwritten journaling.

TOTAL TIME TO SCRAPLIFT:

## 30 minutes

**Dragon Land** by Nicole Samuels. **Supplies** *Cardstock:* Bazzill Basics Paper; *Patterned paper, chipboard accents, letter stickers, and rub-on dotted lines:* Pink Paislee; *Rub-on letters:* American Crafts; *Mini letter stickers, word stickers and felt star:* Making Memories; *Button:* BasicGrey; *Sequins:* Studio Calico; *Other:* Embroidery floss.

### INSTRUCTIONS

1. Use strips of patterned paper and border stickers to create line across middle of cardstock background. Attach three vertical photos cropped to 4" x 2½" above line, and three more below line.

2. Create title with rub-on and letter stickers on chipboard accent. Top with chipboard star embellished with button and felt star tied with floss. Add sequin flowers.

3. Journal in strips with word and letter stickers. Finish with rub-on dotted lines.

## from the pantry

☐ 1 sheet cardstock

☐ 1 sheet patterned paper

☐ 2 sets letter stickers (1 mini)

☐ 1 set rub-on letters

☐ 1 set rub-on dotted lines

☐ 2 chipboard accents (label and star)

☐ 8 word stickers

☐ 2 border-strip stickers

☐ 1 computer font

☐ Embroidery floss

☐ 6 photographs

## just add

☐ 1 felt star

☐ 1 button

☐ Sequins

TOTAL TIME TO SCRAPLIFT:

## 30 minutes

### from the pantry

- ☐ 5 sheets cardstock
- ☐ 3 sheets patterned paper (swirl and 2 dot)
- ☐ 2 brads
- ☐ 2 computer fonts
- ☐ 11 photographs

### just add

- ☐ 1 felt flower
- ☐ 2 photo turns
- ☐ 1 button

**Clam Gulch** by Courtney Kelly. **Supplies** *Photo-collage software:* FotoFusion, LumaPix; *Cardstock:* Bazzill Basics Paper; *Patterned paper:* Doodlebug Design, Heidi Swapp for Advantus and Scenic Route; *Felt flower and button:* Making Memories; *Photo turns:* American Crafts; *Brads:* KI Memories; *Fonts:* Century Gothic and King; *Other:* Corner-rounder punch.

## make it (even) easier!

Crop and adhere your photos manually rather than using collage software.

I love everything about this city; even the name makes me feel more Alaskan. And if ever there was that special place in my life that just heals me, it's here. The second I step out of the car every stress I feel, every negative thought, any sadness in my life slips away. This is our place. We run crazy here, it doesn't matter how cold it is, I take off my shoes, roll up my pants, splash in the water, run in the sand chasing after the kids, and of course never have my camera more than an arms reach away. The kids run along the shore, enjoying the warm and cozy 40-45 degree water. We have races, spot birds, holler at the wind, and hey, even bust out the clam shovel. Of course we have never actually found a live clam at Clam Gulch, but I have an inkling that we will someday.

## Clam Gulch
July 26, 2008

## INSTRUCTIONS

1 Create photo collages using collage software. Mat on white cardstock and adhere to blue background.

2 Add strips of patterned paper, rounding select corners. Type journaling and title on computer and print. Round select corners and attach to layout.

3 Add yellow strip for accent. Attach photo turns with brads. Finish with flower and button.

TOTAL TIME TO SCRAPLIFT:

# 1 hour

## from the pantry

☐ 10 sheets patterned paper (4 floral, 2 dot, 2 striped and 2 cream)

☐ 1 set letter stickers

☐ 1 set letter stamps

☐ 1 ribbon scrap

☐ 4 sticker accents

☐ 2 yards rickrack (pink and red)

☐ 1 stamp

☐ 2 inkpads

☐ 2 tubes paint

☐ 4 photographs 4×6

## just add

☐ Yarn

☐ 2 buttons

## make it (even) easier!

**Too busy to stamp? Try stickers instead.**

### INSTRUCTIONS

*Note: Although Rebecca produced her layout digitally, our instructions explain how to create it using traditional supplies.*

1   Position three vertical and one horizontal photo on background paper. Add strips of various patterned papers along top of horizontal photo and below entire photo block. Attach two strips of rickrack beneath patterned-paper border. Place two buttons to left of rickrack.

2   Add splashes of paint at top left and bottom right of design. Apply letter stickers for top half of title. Stamp letters for bottom word of title and cut out. Position party hat embellishment and candle stickers in bottom-right corner. Tie bow and attach.

3   Stamp image on photo and background with two different ink colors, and align photo to background image. Punch holes in striped paper and loop yarn through, tying bows on each end.

**Birthday Bites** by Rebecca Hilleary.
**Supplies** *Software:* Adobe Photoshop
Elements 6.0; *Digital background paper
(white):* Sweet Cherry Pie by Nancie
Rowe Janitz; *Digital patterned paper:*
Rainbow Room by Kim Christensen;
*Digital letters:* Berry-Licious Alphas
by Jacque Larson (purple) and
Marker Madness by Kim Christensen
(multicolored); *Digital trims:* String-
A-Ling III (yarn) and Sunday Morning
(orange bow) by Natalie Braxton;
*Digital candle and party hat:* Make a
Wish by Kate Hadfield; *Digital rickrack,
brush and buttons:* Berry Sweet by
Gypsy Chick; *Digital glitter paint:* Sweet
Sensation by Lori Barnhurst.

# HOW TO CREATE A DUAL-COLOR
# STAMPED IMAGE WITH MASKING

❶ Determine the placement
of your image and stamp it
onto your background.

❷ Line up the photo and
place the transparency
next to and underneath it,
covering the cardstock.

❸ Position the stamp
exactly in its original spot
and stamp with a different
color of ink. Remove the
transparency to reveal a
dual-colored image.

TOTAL TIME TO SCRAPLIFT:

1
hour

## from the pantry

☐  1 sheet cardstock

☐  3 sheets patterned paper
    (green and 2 teal)

☐  2 sets letter stickers

☐  2 chipboard accents

☐  ½ yard ribbon

☐  1 rub-on border

☐  Embroidery floss

☐  2 pens

☐  1 computer font

☐  6 photographs

## just add

☐  Playing cards

☐  3 buttons

☐  2 felt accents (corner and border)

**Papa, Elijah & the Old Maid** by Cindy Tobey. **Supplies** *Patterned paper, buttons, felt accents, ribbon and rub-on border:* Fancy Pants Designs; *Chipboard accents and stickers:* American Crafts; *Embroidery floss:* DMC; *Playing cards:* ThinkFun, Inc.; *Ink:* Clearsnap; *Pens:* American Crafts (black) and Uni-ball Signo, Newell Rubbermaid (white); *Font:* Myriad Pro Condensed; *Other:* Staples.

## make it
## (even) easier!

Use adhesive to attach elements
in place of staples and floss.

You had played with all of Daddy's old toys and were starting to complain of boredom when Grandma suggested playing a game, Old Maid. Since this was your first time playing this game you enlisted Papa to be on "your team," you and Papa against Grandma, the boys against the girl. You were so animated and would squeal with delight *every* time you chose a card that *wasn't* the Old Maid. You loved playing with Papa and it was great watching the two of you connect and have so much fun together. We laughed a lot that day and you learned that you love Old Maid, *especially* playing it with Papa. I thought about buying you some Old Maid cards, but then decided it would be more fun and special for you if we save playing this game for visits with Papa and Grandma. Papa has always been cool to you because of his big tractors and barns, but now I think you've added his rockin' Old Maid playing skills to the list. You have one seriously cool Papa!

# papa, elijah, & the OLD MAID

OLD MAID

## INSTRUCTIONS

1 Attach playing cards to top edge of aqua background. Create journaling on computer and print on aqua paper. Mat or print some photos with white border and arrange on layout, backing one with playing card. Add journaling column and another playing card.

2 Apply ribbon on edge of aqua paper and attach to green background. Staple ribbon and felt border along bottom edge of aqua paper. Add rub-on border to left edge of layout.

3 Create title with letter stickers. Draw white border around black letters. Finish with buttons and chipboard accents.

TOTAL TIME TO SCRAPLIFT:

## 30 minutes

## from the pantry

- ☐ 1 sheet cardstock
- ☐ 2 sheets patterned paper (striped and ledger)
- ☐ 1 set letter stickers (and numerals)
- ☐ 1 pen
- ☐ 1 brad
- ☐ 3 photographs

## just add

- ☐ 2 die cuts (border and label)
- ☐ 1 journaling card
- ☐ 1 felt flower

### INSTRUCTIONS

1 Round corners of lined background paper. Crop three photos to same size and attach along line on background. Cut border strip and striped paper to same length of photo block. Round corners and attach.

2 Position journaling card and label, and handwrite text.

3 Add letter and number stickers for title and date. Finish with flower and brad.

## make it (even) easier!

Create your own journaling card with lined paper and a border sticker.

**House 4 Sale** by Ruth Dealey. **Supplies** *Cardstock:* Bazzill Basics Paper; *Patterned paper, border die cut, label die cut and journaling card:* October Afternoon; *Felt flower:* Maya Road; *Letter stickers:* BasicGrey; *Corner-rounder punch:* EK Success; *Brad:* Heidi Swapp for Advantus; *Pen:* Pigma Micron, Sakura.

## bonus project

**Ruth put her scraps to good use and made this handsome card.**

**Happy Father's Day** by Ruth Dealey. **Supplies** *Cardstock:* Bazzill Basics Paper; *Patterned paper:* October Afternoon (striped and dot) and Scenic Route (grid) *Journaling card:* October Afternoon; *Flower:* Prima; *Brad:* Dovecraft; *Corner-rounder punch:* EK Success; *Rub-ons:* Heidi Grace Designs; *Other:* Dimensional adhesive.

**Fall Play** by Brenda Hurd. **Supplies** *Cardstock and scallop border:* Bazzill Basics Paper; *Patterned paper:* Cosmo Cricket; *Felt branch:* Fancy Pants Designs; *Leaves:* Prima; *Letter stickers:* BasicGrey; *Twine trim:* The Scarlet Lime; *Journaling stamp and buttons:* Autumn Leaves; *Ink:* Close To My Heart; *Pen:* Zig Writer, EK Success; *Other:* Staples and thread.

## from the pantry

☐   1 sheet cardstock

☐   3 sheets patterned paper

☐   1 set letter stickers

☐   ½ yard trim

☐   1 journaling stamp

☐   1 inkpad

☐   1 pen

☐   Thread

☐   3 photographs

## just add

☐   1 felt tree branch

☐   5 buttons

☐   7 silk leaves

## make it
## (even) easier!

Instead of stitching, staple ribbons
and papers, or use adhesive.

## INSTRUCTIONS

**1** Stitch dot-paper circle to cardstock background. Layer strips of yellow paper, scallop border and striped paper atop circle. Attach photos overlapping striped paper.

**2** Staple trim along bottom edge of photos. Affix felt branch to layout and add leaves. Apply buttons to scallop.

**3** Stamp journaling circle. Mat and apply to layout. Handwrite journaling and add letter stickers for title.

TOTAL TIME TO SCRAPLIFT:

# 1 hour

## from the pantry

- ☐ 2 sheets cardstock
- ☐ 5 sheets patterned paper (3 swirl and 2 red)
- ☐ 1 set letter stickers
- ☐ 1 sheet rub-ons
- ☐ 2 chipboard accents
- ☐ 2 yards ribbon (red and green)
- ☐ ½ yard green leaf trim
- ☐ 1 decorative brad
- ☐ Embroidery floss
- ☐ 1 inkpad
- ☐ 1 tube paint
- ☐ 1 pen
- ☐ 1 computer font
- ☐ 5 photographs

## just add

- ☐ Rhinestones
- ☐ 2 silk flowers
- ☐ 1 transparency

**Fashionista** by Kathi Kirkland. **Supplies** *Cardstock:* Archiver's (white) and Bazzill Basics Paper (green); *Patterned paper:* American Crafts (green) and BasicGrey (reds); *Chipboard:* American Crafts (letters) and KI Memories (shapes); *Rub-ons:* BasicGrey; *Ribbon:* Making Memories (green) and May Arts (sheer red, green leaves); *Fabric brad:* K&Company; *Transparency:* Inkadinkado; *Rhinestones:* Darice (small red), Kaisercraft (small green) and Prima (large); *Silk flowers:* Heidi Swapp for Advantus; *Scallop border punch:* Fiskars; *Font:* Georgia.

## make it (even) easier!

Use premade borders or patterned-paper strips instead of punching or cutting by hand.

## INSTRUCTIONS

1 Create journaling on computer and mat on patterned paper. Attach to left side of layout. Apply a row of photos, one somewhat larger and extending beyond top and bottom of row. Add title to top of journaling block and extending to right above photos.

2 Cut along patterned-paper design to create green strip. Layer with punched red/white paper strip along bottom of layout. Add rub-ons and transparency to layout in various places, accenting with rhinestones.

3 Layer ribbons atop green strip. Create flower accent with silk flowers, chipboard accent, green trim and fabric brad. Finish with chipboard accent at top of journaling block.

TOTAL TIME TO SCRAPLIFT:

## 45
minutes

## from the pantry

- ☐ 2 sheets cardstock
- ☐ 4 sheets patterned paper (striped, dot and 2 floral)
- ☐ 4 chipboard flourish accents
- ☐ 1 definition sticker
- ☐ 1 pen
- ☐ 5 photographs **4×6**

## just add

- ☐ 1 set chipboard letters
- ☐ 5 decorative flower centers
- ☐ 1 journaling card die cut

**Easter Bliss** by Amy Wheeler. **Supplies** *Cardstock:* Bazzill Basics Paper; *Patterned paper and journaling card:* October Afternoon; *Chipboard letters, definition sticker, chipboard flourishes and paint:* Making Memories; *Pen:* American Crafts; *Other:* Decorative accents for flower centers.

## make it
(even) easier!

Try a page kit. With the items
already coordinated for you,
all you have to do is add photos!

## INSTRUCTIONS

1  Position photos on background and adhere to page. Cut various strips of patterned papers and arrange around photos.

2  Handwrite journaling and attach to layout. Apply title.

3  Cut flowers from patterned paper and add brads or epoxy stickers for centers. Apply to layout with chipboard flourishes.

TOTAL TIME TO SCRAPLIFT:

1
hour

☐  3 sheets cardstock

☐  3 sheets patterned paper
    (plaid)

☐  2 sets letter stickers

☐  3 chipboard accents

☐  3 brads

☐  1 pen

☐  1 computer font

☐  Embroidery floss

☐  5 photographs  4×6

just add

☐  6 buttons

☐  2 felt embellishments (swirl
    and border)

☐  3 crocheted flowers

make it
(even) easier!

Eliminate the hand-stitching, and use a shaped
patterned paper to replicate the bracket.

**Free Falling** by Lisa Dorsey. **Supplies** *Software:* Adobe Photoshop Elements; *Cardstock:* Bazzill Basics Paper (orange) and Making Memories (teal); *Patterned paper:* BasicGrey; *Felt accents:* Fancy Pants Designs; *Digital label (altered):* Swank Labels by Jennifer Pebbles (large left bracket); *Chipboard letters:* Cloud 9 Design, Fiskars; *Crocheted flowers:* Handmade by Mary Jackson; *Brads:* American Crafts; *Buttons:* Jesse James & Co.; *Embroidery floss:* DMC; *Pen:* Zig Writer, EK Success; *Font:* Century Gothic.

As the leaves start falling to
the ground, you both find it
hard to resist the urge to
jump, crunch and fall in them.

## INSTRUCTIONS

1 Mat plaid paper on teal cardstock. Create left bracket digitally and print on strip of plaid paper. Cut out and apply to layout. Arrange photos.

2 Adhere felt swirl to layout and accent with buttons, flowers and brads. Create journaling on computer and cut into strips. Hand-stitch on buttons, along flourish and on a few photos.

3 Cut out orange letters and apply letter stickers for title. Finish with felt border.

TOTAL TIME TO SCRAPLIFT:

1
hour

## from the pantry

- ☐ 4 sheets cardstock
- ☐ 2 sheets patterned paper (striped)
- ☐ 1 set letter stickers
- ☐ 1 piece sticker tape
- ☐ 4 chipboard accents
- ☐ 1 adhesive badge
- ☐ 1 inkpad
- ☐ 1 ribbon scrap
- ☐ Thread
- ☐ 1 pen
- ☐ 1 computer font
- ☐ 5 photographs

## just add

- ☐ 1 journaling spot
- ☐ 1 set acrylic letters
- ☐ Toothpicks

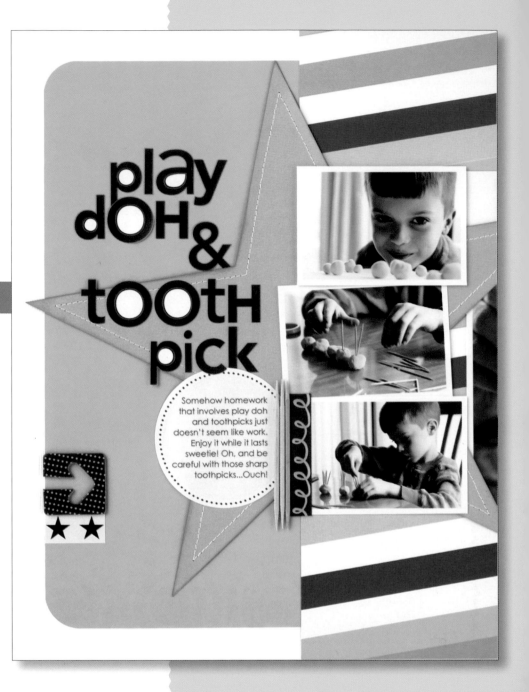

play dOH & tOOTH pick

Somehow homework that involves play doh and toothpicks just doesn't seem like work. Enjoy it while it lasts sweetie! Oh, and be careful with those sharp toothpicks...Ouch!

## INSTRUCTIONS

1 Attach striped paper to cardstock background. Add green cardstock block to left page, rounding outer corners. Position two vertical photos on striped paper.

2 Print enlarged star symbol on tan cardstock. Cut out and attach to layout with machine stitching. Use computer to print on journaling spot. Apply to layout. Staple on acrylic letters. Attach letter stickers.

3 Place three small photos atop star. Add toothpicks, chipboard, ribbon and other embellishments.

Play Doh & Toothpick Math by Cindy Tobey. **Supplies** *Cardstock:* Bazzill Basics Paper (white) and WorldWin (tan); *Patterned paper and adhesive badge:* American Crafts; *Ribbon:* Love, Elsie for KI Memories; *Chipboard accents:* American Crafts (arrow and white stars) and Provo Craft (kraft star); *Stickers:* Doodlebug Design (letters) and Heidi Swapp for Advantus (tape); *Journaling spot:* Heidi Swapp for Advantus; *Acrylic letters:* Autumn Leaves; *Corner-rounder punch:* EK Success; *Ink:* Clearsnap; *Font:* Century Gothic; *Other:* Staples, thread and toothpicks.

## make it (even) easier!

Add your own handwriting to the journaling spot and sketch your own star instead of using your computer.

## bonus project

With a few leftovers, Cindy whipped up this sensational card!

**Hi** by Cindy Tobey. **Supplies** *Cardstock:* Bazzill Basics Paper (white) and WorldWin (tan); *Patterned paper:* American Crafts; *Journaling spot:* Heidi Swapp for Advantus; *Ribbon:* Love, Elsie for KI Memories; *Letter stickers:* Doodlebug Design; *Corner-rounder punch:* EK Success; *Pinking-edge scissors:* Gingher; *Ink:* Clearsnap.

## 45
minutes

## from the pantry

- ☐ 5 sheets cardstock
- ☐ 2 sheets patterned paper
- ☐ 1 set letter stickers
- ☐ 11 brads (various)
- ☐ 2 stamps
- ☐ 2 inkpads
- ☐ 1 set rub-on letters
- ☐ 1 rub-on accent
- ☐ 4 ribbon scraps
- ☐ Thread
- ☐ 1 pen
- ☐ 9 photographs

## just add

- ☐ 1 vintage postage stamp
- ☐ 2 buttons

**Just a Little Obsessed** by Heidi Sonboul. **Supplies** *Cardstock:* Bazzill Basics Paper; *Patterned paper:* Scenic Route (school lines) and Webster's Pages (green); *Ribbon:* Bo-Bunny Press (pink dot) and Bobbin Ribbon (yellow, green and white); *Letter stickers:* Creative Café (brown) and Heidi Swapp for Advantus (white); *Brads:* Making Memories; *Rub-on:* 7gypsies (fleur-de-lis); *Stamps:* Purple Onion Stamps (pointing finger) and Unity Stamps (butterfly); *Embossing powder:* Ranger Industries; *Buttons:* Creative Imaginations; *Other:* Vintage postage stamp and thread.

## make it
## (even) easier!

Skip the white mat and apply the
photo block right to the layout.

## INSTRUCTIONS

**1** Cut 15 2½" x 3½" blocks out of photos and patterned paper. Decorate with stamps, brads or various embellishments, and mat all on white cardstock. Attach to background paper.

**2** Handwrite journaling and add machine-stitching in select places.

**3** Create title with letter stickers. Add a few more stamps or embellishments as final touches.

TOTAL TIME TO SCRAPLIFT:

1 hour

from the pantry

- ☐ 9 sheets patterned paper (2 vintage, 2 blue, 2 dot, pink, striped and shaped)
- ☐ 1 set letter stickers
- ☐ 1 sheet rub-on swirls
- ☐ 4 flower stickers
- ☐ 1 computer font
- ☐ Embroidery floss
- ☐ 12 photographs

## just add

- ☐ 1 rhinestone
- ☐ 1 numeral embellishment
- ☐ 1 die-cut tag

## make it (even) easier!

Use a pen to imitate the look of stitching.

**Wish** by Rebecca Hilleary. **Supplies** *Software:* Adobe Photoshop Elements 6.0; *Digital patterned paper, butterfly brush, bow, letters (altered) and flowers:* Sakura Spring by Paint the Moon Designs; *Digital half-circle paper:* Half Cuts #2 by Amy Wolff; *Digital bracket notebook paper:* Berry Sweet by Gypsy Chick; *Digital stitching:* Brotherly Love by Emily Farnworth; *Digital "3":* Sweet Sensation by Lori Barnhurst; *Font:* Love Letter TW.

## INSTRUCTIONS

*Note: Although Rebecca created her layout digitally, our instructions explain how to create it using traditional supplies.*

1 Punch or crop photos and patterned paper to 2½" squares and mat in grid pattern on blue paper, with striped strip on left end. Attach to layout with half-circle of patterned paper beneath right end.

2 Apply white rub-ons to top-right and bottom-left corners of design. Add stitching atop rub-ons and along top and side corners. Journal on tag and attach to layout.

3 Embellish numeral with rhinestone and add to layout. Affix title and accent with flowers. Finish with bow on striped strip.

TOTAL TIME TO SCRAPLIFT:

## 45
minutes

## from the pantry

- ☐ 2 sheets cardstock
- ☐ 3 sheets patterned paper (striped, grid and grungy)
- ☐ 2 sets letter stickers
- ☐ 1 rub-on border
- ☐ 1 chipboard flower
- ☐ 1 rub-on flower
- ☐ 1 ribbon scrap
- ☐ 1 photo corner
- ☐ 1 brad
- ☐ Embroidery floss
- ☐ 1 inkpad
- ☐ 1 tube paint      ☐ 1 computer font
- ☐ 1 pen             ☐ 4 photographs

## just add

- ☐ 3 buttons         ☐ 1 paper border
- ☐ 3 felt flowers

**Turkey with Legs** by Cindy Tobey. **Supplies** *Cardstock:* Bazzill Basics Paper; *Patterned paper, buttons, chipboard, felt, ribbon and rub-on:* Fancy Pants Designs; *Paper border:* Doodlebug Design; *Brad:* Queen & Co.; *Photo corner:* Heidi Swapp for Advantus; *Ink:* Clearsnap; *Pen and stickers:* American Crafts; *Font:* Calibri. *Other:* Thread. *Note:* This layout is based on a sketch by Becky Higgins.

## INSTRUCTIONS

1  Print journaling on grid paper and create block with grid paper, torn paper and brown cardstock strips. Attach to background paper. Mat or print some photos with white border and arrange on layout.

2  Add paper border and ribbon to left edge of focal-point photo. Stitch on buttons. Create turkey (see instructions on the next page).

3  Apply title with letter stickers. Add rub-on border to top and bottom of design.

# HOW TO CREATE YOUR OWN TURKEY ACCENT

❶ Sketch turkey body onto patterned paper. Cut out and ink edges.

❷ Cut chipboard bloom in half. Paint gold. Cut two petals from felt bloom.

❸ Add rub-on flower to clear transparency or paper. Cut out, cutting away a few of the petals.

❹ Layer the chipboard, felt and rub-on blossoms. Add final felt blossom (green) and stitch to turkey body.

❺ Finish with brad and red felt. Add bird to page and hand-stitch legs with embroidery floss.

## make it (even) easier!

Handwrite your journaling instead of formatting it on your computer.

TOTAL TIME TO SCRAPLIFT:

## 1 hour

## from the pantry

- ☐ 3 sheets cardstock

- ☐ 1 sheet patterned paper (dot)

- ☐ 2 chipboard accents (swirl and bookplate)

- ☐ 1 border stamp

- ☐ 1 inkpad

- ☐ 1 tube paint

- ☐ 2 pens

- ☐ 7 photographs

## just add

- ☐ 1 set chipboard letters

- ☐ Sand

**Discovering Sand** by Leah LaMontagne. **Supplies** *Cardstock:* Prism Papers; *Patterned paper:* American Crafts; *Chipboard:* Fancy Pants Designs (swirls), Making Memories (letters) and Maya Road (bookplate); *Dot border stamp:* Technique Tuesday; *Ink:* Stampin' Up!; *Paint:* Making Memories; *Pens:* Sakura (black) and Uni-ball Signo, Newell Rubbermaid (white); *Other:* Sand.

## make it (even) easier!

Start by skipping the sand, and try stamping with a pencil eraser if you don't have a dot border stamp.

Grainy, mushy, but not tasty!

7 months old.

4.17.07

Levi

## INSTRUCTIONS

**1** Attach aqua paper to yellow background at an angle. Arrange photos in cluster along middle of layout.

**2** Cut sections out of patterned paper for accents and attach behind photos. Write journaling along top and bottom of photo block.

**3** Mix sand into paint. Paint chipboard letters and accents, and add to layout. Stamp border and finish with lettering.

TOTAL TIME TO SCRAPLIFT:

## 30
minutes

### from the pantry

- ☐ 4 sheets cardstock

- ☐ 4 sheets patterned paper (striped, grungy and 2 gold)

- ☐ 1 set dimensional letter stickers

- ☐ ½ yard ribbon

- ☐ 3 brads

- ☐ 1 pen

- ☐ 5 photographs

### just add

- ☐ 1 journaling spot die cut

- ☐ 1 machine die cut (pirate flag)

- ☐ 1 piece black chipboard

**READ AT YOUR OWN RISK**

This pirate ship float was a great find @ only $20! You and Madison & Cassidy had the best time @ Mimaw & Paw's pool pretending to be pirates with Daddy! $20 well spent!

**Argh!** by Kelly Noel. **Supplies** *Cardstock and ribbon:* Bazzill Basics Paper; *Patterned paper and die cuts:* Cosmo Cricket; *Letter stickers, brads and pen:* American Crafts; *Chipboard:* Heidi Swapp for Advantus; *Digital craft cutter:* QuicKutz.

## make it
## (even) easier!

Use a pirate embellishment or
clip art in place of a die cut.

## INSTRUCTIONS

1 Center and attach gold patterned paper on background cardstock. Place a strip of ribbon on left end of paper. Hand-cut a "wave" from blue patterned paper and adhere to bottom of layout.

2 Group and mat photos in two blocks, leaving room for title on right-hand mat. Attach strips of patterned paper and die cut to page. Handwrite journaling.

3 Cut die-cut pirate flag accent from black chipboard. Finish with title and brads.

TOTAL TIME TO SCRAPLIFT:

## 45 minutes

- ☐ 7 sheets cardstock
- ☐ 2 sheets patterned paper (dot)
- ☐ Thread
- ☐ 5 photographs

### just add

- ☐ 2 sets letter die cuts
- ☐ Photo-corner die cuts

**Father's Day** by Shaunte Wadley. **Supplies** *Cardstock:* Bazzill Basics Paper (green, yellow) and Prism Papers (brown, rust and blue); *Patterned paper:* Bo-Bunny Press; *Die cuts:* Biography (monogram letters and date), Diesel (title letters) and photo corners, QuicKutz; *Die cutter:* QuicKutz; *Circle punch:* Fiskars; *Other:* Thread.

## make it (even) easier!

Use letter stickers or a computer-generated title instead of a die-cut tool.

## INSTRUCTIONS

1 Mat dot paper on brown cardstock background. Attach artwork to inner edges of 10" x 2½" strips of green cardstock.

2 Use die-cut tool to create date, title and monogram letters. Mount monograms on punched circles backed by red cardstock rectangle and adhere next to drawings. Finish strips with small photos.

3 Use die-cut tool to create photo corners and add to pictures. Back title with large cardstock arrow and create date tab. Attach. Finish by sewing around perimeter of layout.

TOTAL TIME TO SCRAPLIFT:

0 15 30 45

## 30 minutes

### from the pantry

- ☐ 1 sheet cardstock

- ☐ 3 sheets patterned paper (circle, lined and die-cut)

- ☐ 2 sets letter stickers

- ☐ 1 rub-on accent

- ☐ 1 ribbon scrap

- ☐ 1 decorative brad

- ☐ 1 pen

- ☐ Embroidery floss

- ☐ 2 photographs 4×6

### just add

- ☐ 3 die cuts (stamps and label)

- ☐ 3 buttons

- ☐ 1 felt heart

## make it (even) easier!

Replace the embellishment cluster
on the left with a third photo.

**Berry Sweet** by Nicole Samuels. **Supplies** *Cardstock:* Bazzill Basics Paper; *Patterned paper:* Making Memories (green circle and die-cut edged) and Studio Calico (vintage memo); *Letter stickers:* BasicGrey; *Brad, red buttons, die cuts, ribbon and chipboard letter stickers:* Making Memories; *Flower buttons:* KI Memories; *Felt heart and pen:* American Crafts; *Other:* Rub-on.

### INSTRUCTIONS

1 Attach pieces of memo paper and circle patterned paper to cardstock background. Align two vertical photos toward right of layout. Add decorative edges from die-cut paper to seam.

2 Layer products to create embellishment cluster on bottom left. Affix label above photos and top with chipboard letters. Apply letter stickers to photo on right.

3 Add small embellishments above title. Journal on memo paper beneath photos.

## make it (even) easier!

Have your developer print the photos with a white border for ready-made mats.

**Last Day of School** by Brenda Carpenter. **Supplies** *Cardstock:* Bazzill Basics Paper; *Patterned paper:* My Mind's Eye; *Chipboard letters:* Heidi Swapp for Advantus; *Die cuts:* Creative Imaginations (green tag) and My Mind's Eye (label); *Buttons:* Buttons Galore; *Stamps:* Hero Arts (owls) and Stampin' Up! ("of"); *Ink:* StazOn, Tsukineko; *Punches:* EK Success (corner rounder) and Stampin' Up! (small circle); *Pinking-edge scissors:* Fiskars; *Ribbon:* Stampin' Up!; *Pen:* American Crafts; *Other:* Thread.

## INSTRUCTIONS

1. Mat red cardstock background on aqua cardstock. Punch patterned-paper corners and attach. Adhere strip of plaid paper, cardstock "grass" (cut with pinking-edge scissors) and hand-cut tree trunk to layout.

2. Attach ribbon to tag and add to layout. Place and adhere photos, overlapping some slightly. Add title letters. Stamp owl and "of" on cardstock. Cut out owl, punch out word and apply to layout.

3. Hand-cut tree from striped paper. Sew onto layout with buttons. Finish with label and handwritten journaling.

**TOTAL TIME TO SCRAPLIFT:**

## 45 minutes

## from the pantry

- ☐ 3 sheets cardstock
- ☐ 3 sheets patterned paper (striped, dot and plaid)
- ☐ 1 set letter stickers
- ☐ 1 set letter stamps
- ☐ 1 owl stamp
- ☐ 1 inkpad
- ☐ 1 ribbon scrap
- ☐ 1 pen
- ☐ Thread
- ☐ 3 photographs

## just add

- ☐ 2 die cuts (tag and label)
- ☐ 6 buttons

## bonus project

Brenda used coordinating papers for this fun card.

**Happy Birthday** by Brenda Carpenter. **Supplies** *Cardstock:* Bazzill Basics Paper; *Patterned paper:* My Mind's Eye; *Die cuts:* My Mind's Eye (blue strip and scallop border); *Stamps:* Stampin' Up!; *Ink:* StazOn, Tsukineko; *Other:* Label sticker and thread.

TOTAL TIME TO SCRAPLIFT:

# 30
## minutes

## from the pantry

- ☐ 3 sheets cardstock
- ☐ 1 set letter stickers
- ☐ 1 set rub-on letters
- ☐ 2 rub-on accents
- ☐ 2 rhinestone brads
- ☐ 1 date stamp
- ☐ 1 inkpad
- ☐ 1 computer font
- ☐ Thread
- ☐ 4 photographs 4×6

**October** by Lisa Dickinson. **Supplies** *Cardstock:* Bazzill Basics Paper; *Acrylic shapes:* Maya Road; *Rub-ons:* American Crafts (letters) and Hambly Screen Prints (tree and leaf); *Chipboard letter stickers:* Heidi Swapp for Advantus; *Felt flowers:* American Crafts; *Rhinestone brads:* Spare Parts; *Font:* Pea Yar Yar; *Other:* Thread, ink, staple and date stamp.

## just add

- ☐ 3 felt flowers
- ☐ 2 acrylic shapes

## make it
## (even) easier!

Instead of mixing two colors of cardstock for
the background, just stick to one shade.

## INSTRUCTIONS

1 Cut a 4" x 12" piece off the top of two coordinating pieces of cardstock. Print computer journaling on one of the larger pieces. Create background by switching the top pieces so the diagonal sections are the same color. Mat four 4" x 6" vertical photos on white cardstock, leaving extra margins at right and left edges. Tear along left edge and attach to background.

2 Apply rub-on letters to acrylic notepaper shape. Staple to layout and add rub-on leaf, felt flowers and brad.

3 Create title with calendar shape, felt flower, rub-on tree, brad and chipboard letters. Finish by stitching around perimeter of layout. Add date stamp.

TOTAL TIME TO SCRAPLIFT:

## 45
minutes

### from the pantry

☐ 3 sheets cardstock

☐ 1 sheet patterned paper
(honeycomb)

☐ Embroidery floss

☐ 1 pen

☐ 4 photographs 4×6

### just add

☐ 1 set letter die cuts

☐ 11 buttons

☐ 3 silk flowers

**Got Mud?** by Davinie Fiero. **Supplies** *Cardstock:* Bazzill Basics Paper; *Patterned paper:* BasicGrey (floral) and My Mind's Eye (blue); *Flowers:* Petaloo; *Letter die cuts:* Li'l Davis Designs; *Buttons:* Autumn Leaves; *Pen:* Uni-ball Signo, Newell Rubbermaid; *Other:* Embroidery floss.

## make it
## (even) easier!

Substitute a border strip or a
piece of ribbon for the stitching.

mud?

mound of dirt, the garden hose, and the freedom to explore her world.

## INSTRUCTIONS

1 Position four photos on brown background cardstock, alternating horizontal and vertical photos. Add strips of torn patterned paper and blue cardstock along bottom of photos.

2 Handwrite journaling. Attach letter die cuts above and below horizontal photos.

3 Hand-stitch along top of photos. Decorate with buttons and flowers.

TOTAL TIME TO SCRAPLIFT:

# 1 hour

## from the pantry

- ☐ 2 sheets cardstock
- ☐ 2 sheets patterned paper (paisley and floral)
- ☐ 1 set letter stickers
- ☐ 3 chipboard accents
- ☐ 2 border stickers
- ☐ 1 circle stamp
- ☐ 1 inkpad
- ☐ 1 pen
- ☐ 12 photographs

## just add

- ☐ 2 acetate accents
- ☐ 1 wooden tag

## make it (even) easier!

No acetate accents? Use fun floral stickers or chipboard for a similar effect.

**Bonnie Vale** by Kim Arnold. **Supplies** *Software:* Adobe Photoshop CS3; *Cardstock, patterned paper and border stickers:* My Mind's Eye; *Chipboard:* Heidi Swapp for Advantus (letter stickers) and Making Memories (accents); *Wooden tag:* We R Memory Keepers; *Acetate accents:* Heidi Swapp for Advantus; *Scalloped border punch:* Fiskars; *Stamp, ink and pen:* Stampin' Up!.

## INSTRUCTIONS

1 Stamp background pattern on brown cardstock. Attach identical borders made from patterned paper and border stickers to bottom of right page and toward left of left page.

2 Create photo collages using collage software and line up on layout. Embellish with chipboard and acetate accents. Add wooden tag beneath photos on left page.

3 Handwrite journaling on cardstock and cut into strips. Apply to layout and finish with letter stickers for title.

1
hour

## from the pantry

☐ 3 sheets patterned paper (dot, plaid and grid)

☐ 1 set letter stickers

☐ 1 set number stickers (mini)

☐ 1 chipboard bird accent

☐ Brads (various blue)

☐ 4 ribbons (½ yard apiece)

☐ 1 tube paint

☐ Embroidery floss and thread

☐ 1 computer font

☐ 5 photographs

## just add

☐ 2 buttons

☐ 3 felt embellishments (border, frame and corner)

You were so excited to hunt Easter eggs this year. Every time you found one you would show us and squeal with delight. You were so fun to watch. You loved the Bob the Builder toys, money and candy that filled your eggs. But honestly, I think the real thrill for you was the hunt. Next year we definitely need to hide more eggs for you.

**Hunting** by Cindy Tobey. **Supplies** *Patterned paper, buttons, chipboard, felt accents, journaling spot and ribbon:* Fancy Pants Designs; *Brads:* KI Memories (blue glitter) and Queen & Co. (all others); *Number stickers:* Li'l Davis Designs; *Paint:* Making Memories; *Font:* Lucida Console; *Other:* Embroidery floss, thread and staples.

## make it (even) easier!

Save time by using a premade bird embellishment and patterned papers instead of ribbon.

## INSTRUCTIONS

**1** Attach photos of various sizes to background paper. Add two blocks of patterned paper to left page. Staple ribbons to layout to fill in spaces between photos and papers.

**2** Use computer to print on grid paper. Apply to layout. Stitch edge. Stitch felt scallop border to right side of layout.

**3** Adhere title letters to layout. Paint chipboard bird. When dry, add brads. Finish with buttons, felt corner and date embellishment.

TOTAL TIME TO SCRAPLIFT:

## 45 minutes

### from the pantry

- ☐ 4 sheets cardstock

- ☐ 1 sheet patterned paper (floral)

- ☐ 2 sets letter stickers

- ☐ 2 chipboard brackets

- ☐ 1 computer font

- ☐ 1 decorative brad

- ☐ Embroidery floss

- ☐ Thread

- ☐ 1 pen

- ☐ 5 photographs

### just add

- ☐ 1 paper border

- ☐ 1 button

- ☐ 2 felt butterflies

**Your Happy Ending** by Summer Fullerton. **Supplies** *Cardstock:* Bazzill Basics Paper and Core'dinations; *Patterned paper:* Tinkering Ink; *Felt butterflies:* Jenni Bowlin Studio; *Letter stickers and paper border:* Doodlebug Design; *Chipboard:* American Crafts (brackets) and Scenic Route (letter stickers); *Button:* SEI; *Decorative brad:* Imaginisce; *Embroidery floss:* DMC; *Pen:* Uni-ball Signo, Newell Rubbermaid; *Font:* Traveling Typewriter; *Other:* Adhesive dots and thread.

### INSTRUCTIONS

1 Line up five vertical photos, cropping sides of some, and attach slightly above middle of layout. Add patterned paper and cardstock strips along top and bottom of photo block.

2 Journal on computer and cut into strips. Attach to right of photo block. Create title with letter stickers, chipboard brackets, paper border and brad.

3 Draw dashed lines with white pen and affix butterflies to layout with adhesive dots. Sew button to patterned paper.

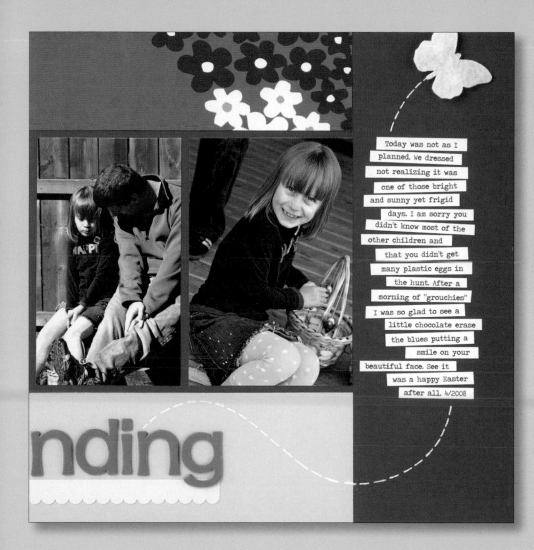

Today was not as I planned. We dressed not realizing it was one of those bright and sunny yet frigid days. I am sorry you didn't know most of the other children and that you didn't get many plastic eggs in the hunt. After a morning of "grouchies" I was so glad to see a little chocolate erase the blues putting a smile on your beautiful face. See it was a happy Easter after all. 4/2008

nding

## make it (even) easier!

Replace the journaling strips with a block of journaling.

## bonus project

What a darling card! Use up your leftovers creatively, like Summer did here.

**Thanks** by Summer Fullerton.
**Supplies** *Cardstock:* Bazzill Basics Paper and Core'dinations; *Patterned paper:* Tinkering Ink; *Letter stickers:* Doodlebug Design.

TOTAL TIME TO SCRAPLIFT:

## 45 minutes

## from the pantry

- ☐ 4 sheets cardstock
  (2 laser-cut)

- ☐ 6 sheets patterned paper
  (3 dot, 2 floral and 1 leaf)

- ☐ 3 sets letter stickers

- ☐ 11 brads (various)

- ☐ 1 inkpad

- ☐ Embroidery floss

- ☐ 1 pen

- ☐ 3 photographs

## just add

- ☐ 3 felt flowers

- ☐ 1 stick pin

## make it (even) easier!

Use a large punch for fast patterned-paper squares!

**My Sweet Boy** by Allison Davis. **Supplies** *Cardstock and brads:* Bazzill Basics Paper; *Specialty cardstock:* KI Memories; *Patterned paper:* Scenic Route; *Letter stickers:* American Crafts ("Sweet" and "Boy") and Doodlebug Design ("My"); *Felt flowers and pin:* Fancy Pants Designs; *Ink:* Color-Box, Clearsnap; *Embroidery floss:* DMC; *Pen:* Sakura.

Drew is the sweetest little boy. Every time he sees flowers he picks them for me. I get a sweaty wad of flowers almost every day. If he keeps this up, the girls will love him. My sweet boy.

## INSTRUCTIONS

1 Cut and ink squares of patterned paper and attach to cardstock background. Hand-stitch around patterned-paper squares.

2 Position photographs and adhere. Create embellishment clusters with laser-cut cardstock and various accents.

3 Add letter stickers for title, and handwrite journaling.

TOTAL TIME TO SCRAPLIFT:

# 45
minutes

## from the pantry

☐ 3 sheets cardstock

☐ 7 sheets patterned paper
(purple, blue, green, yellow,
orange, red and pink)

☐ 3 sets letter stickers

☐ 1 computer font

☐ 7 photogaphs

## just add

☐ 1 transparency sheet

☐ Buttons

**My Colorful World** by Susan Opel. **Supplies** *Cardstock:* Bazzill Basics Paper; *Patterned paper:* Anna Griffin (orange), Carolee's Creations (red), Creative Imaginations (green), Karen Foster Design (purple), KI Memories (blue), My Mind's Eye (yellow) and Pebbles Inc. (pink); *Transparency:* Creative Imaginations; *Letter stickers:* American Crafts ("Colorful"), Doodlebug Design ("My") and Sonburn ("World"); *Font:* Beau; *Other:* Buttons.

## make it
## (even) easier!

Print your journaling on a
transparency or use rub-ons.

## INSTRUCTIONS

**1** Trim photos to same height but varying widths, and mat on black cardstock to fit along top length of layout. Choose patterned paper in coordinating colors and cut to match widths of corresponding photos.

**2** To add journaling, carefully run right side of layout with patterned paper attached through printer. Create title with three different types of black letter stickers.

**3** Add swirl transparency atop certain areas of layout. Apply buttons in matching colors along edge of photos.

TOTAL TIME TO SCRAPLIFT:

## 50 minutes

### from the pantry

- ☐ 3 sheets of cardstock
- ☐ 4 sheets of patterned paper (2 geometric, 1 striped, 1 textured)
- ☐ 3 brads
- ☐ 2 photo corners
- ☐ 1 corner rounder punch
- ☐ 1 pen
- ☐ 1 inkpad
- ☐ 1 punctuation stamp
- ☐ 4 photographs 4×6

### just add

- ☐ 1 circle cutter
- ☐ 1 set of punch-out cardstock letters

**Round & Round** by Miriam Campbell
**Supplies** *Textured cardstock:* Bazzill Basics Paper and KI Memories; *Patterned papers:* Scenic Route Paper Co.; *Brads:* Magic Scraps; *Lettering accents:* Déjà Views by The C-Thru Ruler Co.; *Stamping ink:* Ancient Page, Clearsnap; *"&" rubber stamp:* Impress Rubber Stamps; *Chipboard photo corners:* Chatterbox; *Circle cutter:* Coluzzle, Provo Craft; *Other:* Corner rounder.

"California Adventure"

& round

## make it (even) easier!

You don't need a circle-cutting system to cut large circles. Try using a craft knife, a self-healing mat and the rim of a plastic cereal bowl.

Use letter stickers instead of punch-out cardstock letters for your title.

## INSTRUCTIONS

1 Cut patterned-paper strips 12" wide and stretch them across the two-page spread. Use a corner rounder on the narrow strips.

2 Cut circles with a circle cutter. (Don't be concerned with creating perfectly symmetrical circles.) Start with the outside circle first and then cut the inside hole

off-center. Slip photos through the circles and adhere them to the layout.

3 Add cardstock letters along the curve of the circles. Handwrite on the journaling strips and attach them with brads.

TOTAL TIME TO SCRAPLIFT:

## 45
### minutes

### from the pantry

- ☐ 3 sheets of cardstock
- ☐ 1 sheet of patterned paper (floral)
- ☐ 1 sheet of letter stickers
- ☐ 1 pen
- ☐ 1 computer font
- ☐ 7 photographs

### just add

- ☐ 7 paper flowers
- ☐ 2 word stickers
- ☐ 1 rub-on word

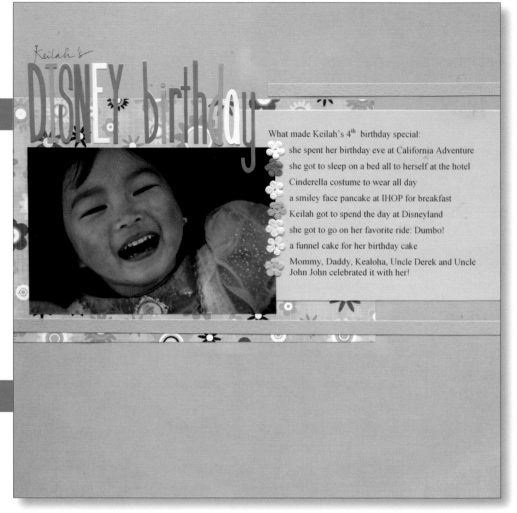

Keilah's

## DISNEY birthday

What made Keilah's 4th birthday special:

she spent her birthday eve at California Adventure

she got to sleep on a bed all to herself at the hotel

Cinderella costume to wear all day

a smiley face pancake at IHOP for breakfast

Keilah got to spend the day at Disneyland

she got to go on her favorite ride: Dumbo!

a funnel cake for her birthday cake

Mommy, Daddy, Kealoha, Uncle Derek and Uncle John John celebrated it with her!

**Disney Birthday** by Nely Fok
**Supplies** *Patterned papers and letter stickers:* Chatterbox; *Paper flowers:* Prima; *Pen:* Pigment Pro, American Crafts; *Computer font:* Times New Roman, Microsoft Word; *Other:* Rub-on word.

## INSTRUCTIONS

1 Adhere a block of patterned paper to a sheet of cardstock. Layer your focal-point photo and journaling over it. Create your title with letter stickers directly above the photo.

2 Group the rest of the photos into a single block, trimming where needed. Place the block on a sheet of cardstock and add strips of patterned paper across the top and bottom of the page.

3 Embellish the page with paper flowers, strips of cardstock, word stickers and a rub-on word.

## 30 minutes

### from the pantry

- ☐ 2 sheets of cardstock
- ☐ 5 strips of patterned paper
  (2 geometric, 2 striped, 1 text)
- ☐ 2 sheets of letter stickers
- ☐ 3 photographs **4×6**

### just add

- ☐ 3 buttons
- ☐ 3 pieces of twine

**The Muddiest Shoe Showdown 2004** by Rachel Ludwig
**Supplies** *Textured cardstock:* Bazzill Basics Paper; *Patterned papers:* Chatterbox (striped and plaid), Mustard Moon (circles) and Autumn Leaves (text); *Letter stickers:* Chatterbox; *Buttons:* Autumn Leaves; *Other:* Twine.

ST SHOE showdown 2004

## INSTRUCTIONS

1 Adhere your photos to the layout, then add patterned-paper strips across the two-page spread.

2 Apply letter stickers to create the title and subtitle.

3 Embellish the layout with buttons tied with twine.

TOTAL TIME TO SCRAPLIFT:

## 45 minutes

### from the pantry

- ☐ 2 sheets of cardstock
- ☐ 1 sheet of patterned paper (striped)
- ☐ 1 pen
- ☐ 3 photographs **4×6**

### just add

- ☐ 1 set of letter stencils
- ☐ 2 circle stickers
- ☐ 1 label tape

## make it (even) easier!

Create your title with letter stickers instead of stencils.

*We celebrated your 6th birthday at home with just us since it was on a weeknight. We had a little cake and lots of presents! Just a little something until your party!*

**birthday girl**

2/17/2005

**Birthday Girl** by Heather Preckel
**Supplies** *Textured cardstock:* Bazzill Basics Paper; *Patterned paper and epoxy stickers:* Autumn Leaves; *Stencil letters:* Making Memories; *Label tape:* Dymo; *Stamping ink:* Ranger Industries; *Pen:* Pigment Pro, American Crafts.

### INSTRUCTIONS

1 Cut a 10" x 8" piece of patterned paper and adhere it to a sheet of cardstock.

2 Mat your focal-point photo and adhere all of the photos to the page.

3 Handwrite your journaling and the first half of the title. Cover the letter stencils with cardstock and arrange them on the page for the second half of the title. Embellish page with sticker gems and label tape.

## 45 minutes

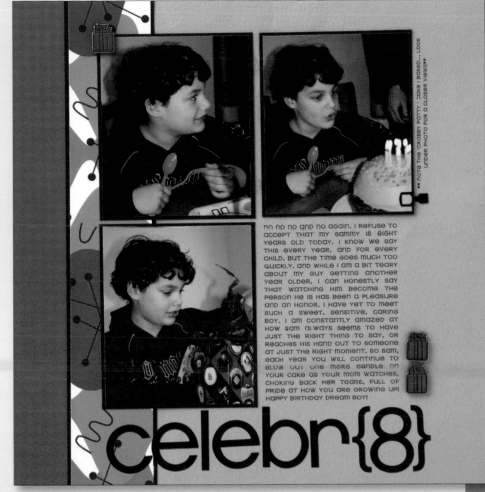

**Celebr{8}** by Renee Foss
**Supplies** *Textured cardstock:* Bazzill Basics Paper; *Patterned papers:* Gin-X, Imagination Project; *Letter stickers:* American Crafts; *Metal charms:* All My Memories; *Small black tab:* 7gypsies; *Plastic photo flips:* Destination Crafts; *Computer font:* SU Joyola, downloaded from the Internet.

### from the pantry

- ☐ 2 sheets of cardstock
- ☐ 2 strips of patterned paper (geometric)
- ☐ 1 computer font
- ☐ 1 sheet of letter stickers
- ☐ 4 photographs (1 hidden)

### just add

- ☐ 3 metal charms
- ☐ 2 plastic photo flips (to create the interactive photo flap)

### INSTRUCTIONS

1 Mat all of the photos and one strip of patterned paper with cardstock.

2 Adhere patterned-paper strips and photos to the page. (For the top-right photo, attach two plastic photo flips on the right side to create a "hidden photo" flap. Add an extra photo and/or journaling underneath the flap.)

3 Add your printed journaling and letter stickers to the layout. Embellish the page with metal charms.

## make it (even) easier!

Don't hide additional photos. Instead, place them in a divided sheet protector and store it in your album directly behind your scrapbook page.

TOTAL TIME TO SCRAPLIFT:

## 30
minutes

## from the pantry

- ☐ 2 sheets of cardstock
- ☐ 1 sheet of letter stickers
- ☐ 1 set of letter stamps
- ☐ 1 inkpad
- ☐ 3 brads
- ☐ 1 date stamp
- ☐ 5 photographs

## just add

- ☐ 3 metal-rimmed tags
- ☐ 1 metal frame

**Pike's Place Market, Seattle** by Rachel Ludwig
**Supplies** *Textured cardstock:* Bazzill Basics Paper; *Letter stickers:* Chatterbox; *Letter stamps:* Fontwerks; *Stamping ink:* Clearsnap and Tsukineko; *Metal-rimmed tags and metal frame:* Making Memories; *Brads:* Die Cuts With a View.

make it
(even) easier!

Instead of using a metal frame
to hold your title, mount it on a
square of cardstock.

INSTRUCTIONS

1  Crop and adhere your photos to span across the two-
page spread.

2  Stamp words on metal-rimmed tags and attach them to
the photos with brads.

3  Stamp the date on the metal frame and adhere it to the
layout. Place letter stickers inside the frame to create a
title. Stamp the subtitle above the sticker title.

# 45 minutes

## from the pantry

- ☐ 1 sheet of cardstock
- ☐ 3 strips of patterned paper (1 geometric, 1 striped, 1 text)
- ☐ 2 pieces of ribbon
- ☐ 1 computer font
- ☐ 1 sheet of rub-on letters
- ☐ 1 sheet of letter stickers
- ☐ 8 staples
- ☐ 3 photographs

## just add

- ☐ 1 decorative brad
- ☐ 1 chipboard accent
- ☐ 1 mini tag

You were just too sweet playing with your Teddy. He wasn't feeling good so you gave him some medicine, sang him a lullaby, and then gave him a hug goodnight. So glad you are learning to care for others, even if he is of the stuffed variety.

sweet **LoVe**

8.29.05

**Sweet Love** by Rhonda Stark
**Supplies** *Software:* Adobe Photoshop, Adobe Systems; *Digital papers, ribbon and chipboard word:* Gina Cabrera and Kristie David, www.theshabbyshoppe.com; *Digital heart brad, stitching and small tag:* Gina Cabrera, www.digitaldesignessentials.com; *Computer font:* AL Uncle Charles, "15 Essentials Fonts" CD, Autumn Leaves.

## INSTRUCTIONS

1 Crop and adhere the patterned-paper strips and photos to the page.

2 Adhere the printed journaling block. Use letter stickers and rub-ons to apply the title to the chipboard tag.

3 Staple or stitch ribbons to the page. Embellish the layout with a decorative brad and a mini tag.

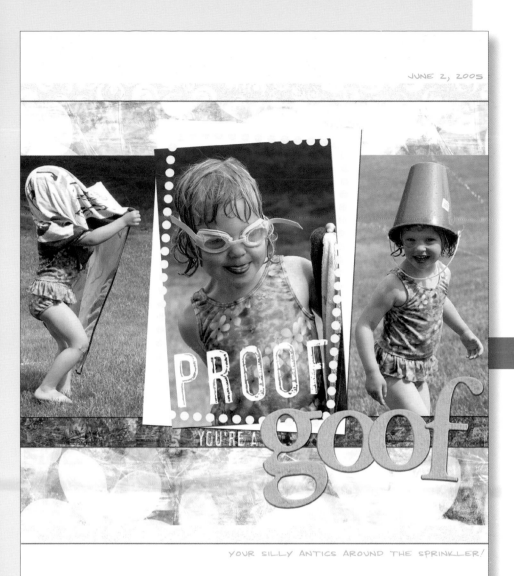

JUNE 2, 2005

PROOF

YOU'RE A goof

YOUR SILLY ANTICS AROUND THE SPRINKLER!

**Goof** by Rhonda Stark
**Supplies** *Software:* Adobe Photoshop, Adobe Systems; *Digital papers:* Kay Miller, *www.designerdigitals.com; Digital stamps:* Rounded Corner, Kate Teague, *www.designerdigitals.com; Digital chipboard letters:* Basic Bare Chipboard Alphas, Katie Pertiet, *www.designerdigitals.com; Computer font:* TIA A Capital Idea by Tia Bennett, *www.designerdigitals.com.*

## from the pantry

- ☐ 1 sheet of cardstock
- ☐ 5 strips of patterned paper (2 geometric, 2 textured, 1 floral)
- ☐ 2 sheets of rub-on letters
- ☐ 1 pen
- ☐ 1 inkpad
- ☐ 3 photographs

## just add

- ☐ 1 rub-on graphic frame
- ☐ 1 set of chipboard letters

### INSTRUCTIONS

1 Crop your patterned paper and photos and place them on the page.

2 Apply a rub-on frame around the focal-point photo. Handwrite your journaling above and below the patterned-paper borders.

3 Ink the chipboard letters and adhere them to the page.

## make it (even) easier!

Line up your photos and mat them on a single sheet of patterned paper instead of using multiple strips.

TOTAL TIME TO SCRAPLIFT:

# 45
## minutes

## from the pantry

☐ 3 sheets of cardstock

☐ 1 sheet of patterned paper (striped)

☐ 1 computer font

☐ 2 pieces of ribbon

☐ 3 photographs

## just add

☐ 1 package of clay letter accents

☐ 1 epoxy sticker

INSTRUCTIONS >

1 Cut angled strips of patterned paper and adhere them to the cardstock.

2 Mat your photos and adhere them to the page. Cut the printed journaling into strips and adhere them to the page.

3 Embellish the page with ribbon and a round epoxy sticker.

**Thank-You Card (from "Scaliwag" scraps)** by Renee Foss
**Supplies** *Textured cardstock:* Bazzill Basics Paper; *Patterned paper and epoxy sticker:* Magic Scraps; *Ribbon:* C.M. Offray & Son; *Stamping ink:* Ranger Industries; *"Thank you" rub-on:* Scenic Route Paper Co.

## bonus project

Don't let your project scraps go to waste! Renee created this darling card from the leftover scraps from her layout.

Scaliwag, rascal...you name it and Sam seems to fit the job description for 'Pirate' [although I'm sure he hasn't plundered for treasure or commandeered a ship...yet]. I had a blast making him up to be a buccaneer this Halloween and he really pulled it off! Dashing with a bit of mischief behind his smile, he looked ready to sail the seven seas in search of adventure!

**Scaliwag** by Renee Foss
**Supplies** *Textured cardstock:* Bazzill Basics Paper; *Patterned paper and epoxy sticker:* Magic Scraps; *Ribbon:* C.M. Offray & Son; *Clay letters:* Li'l Davis Designs; *Computer font:* CK Corral, "Fresh Fonts" CD, *Creating Keepsakes.*

## make it (even) easier!

Use letter stickers instead of clay letters, and handwrite your journaling.

TOTAL TIME TO SCRAPLIFT:

## 30 minutes

### from the pantry

- ☐ 3 sheets of cardstock
- ☐ 2 sheets of rub-on letters
- ☐ 1 pen
- ☐ 1 set of letter/number stamps or date stamp
- ☐ 11 staples
- ☐ 1 photograph **4×6**

### just add

- ☐ 1 set of clear plastic letters
- ☐ 1 set of letter tabs

## make it (even) easier!

Substitute letter stickers for the clear plastic letters.

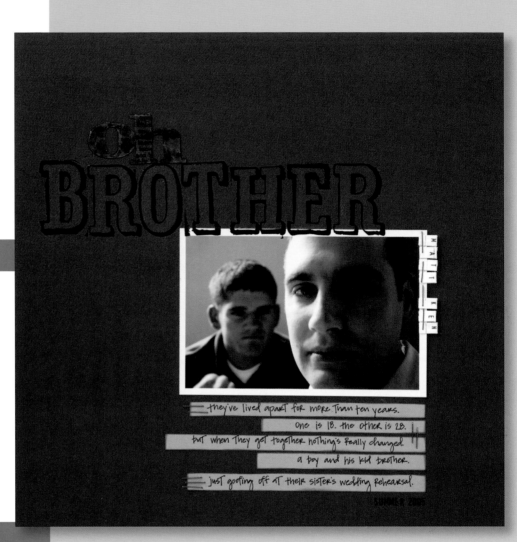

**Oh, Brother** by Laura Kurz
**Supplies** *Rub-on letters:* Autumn Leaves and My Mind's Eye; *Letter tabs:* Autumn Leaves; *Acetate letters:* Heidi Swapp for Advantus; *Staples:* Making Memories; *Other:* Pen.

### INSTRUCTIONS

1 Staple letter tabs to your photo and adhere it to the cardstock.

2 Create the title by applying rub-on letters to the cardstock, overlapping the photo. Adhere rub-ons to the clear plastic letters and adhere them to the page directly above the rub-on letters.

3 Journal on strips of cardstock and attach them to the page with adhesive and staples. Stamp the date under your journaling strips.

TOTAL TIME TO SCRAPLIFT:

## 30 minutes

## recovery
*precious*

SPRING 05

**Precious Recovery** by Laura Kurz
**Supplies** *Letter stickers:* Chatterbox; *Rub-on date:* Autumn Leaves; *"Precious" sticker:* Making Memories; *Computer font:* Georgia, Microsoft Word; *Other:* Stitching, pen and photo corners.

## from the pantry

☐  2 sheets of cardstock

☐  1 sheet of letter stickers

☐  1 set of letter/number stamps or date stamp

☐  1 inkpad

☐  1 pen

☐  2 photo corners

☐  1 computer font

☐  1 photograph  **4×6**

## just add

☐  1 word sticker

☐  stitching

### INSTRUCTIONS

1  Print your journaling on a sheet of cardstock.

2  Adhere the title stickers and the word sticker next to the journaling. Stamp the date underneath the stickers.

3  Stitch photo to a cardstock mat. Leave space on the right edge of the cardstock to write a photo caption. Then, tear the cardstock for a distressed look. Add photo corners on the left edge of the photo before adhering the photo to the layout.

## make it (even) easier!

Love the look of stitching on a layout but don't want to get out the sewing machine? Use rub-on stitches or a rubber stamp instead.

# creativity is served

Despite its clever design, this is not an actual recipe book. Did you notice, however, the large number of food-themed pages? A cool coincidence! Head back inside and check out these flavorful ideas:

**PAGE 14**
**Summer Eats**
by Shannon Brouwer

**PAGE 52**
**Citizen Cupcake**
by Kelly Purkey

**PAGE 60**
**We Love Lobster Rolls**
by Vivian Masket

**PAGE 159**
**The Sweet Life**
by Grace Tolman

**PAGE 174**
**Ice Cream Social**
by Suzy Plantamura

**PAGE 178**
**Dinner, Alaskan Style**
by Courtney Kelly

**PAGE 188**
**Field Trip**
by Stephanie Vetne

**PAGE 230**
**Birthday Bites**
by Rebecca Hilleary

**PAGE 248**
**Turkey with Legs**
by Cindy Tobey

**PAGE 256**
**Berry Sweet**
by Nicole Samuels

We hope the banquet of inspiration in this book has whet your artistic appetite and stimulated your creative juices. Remember, however, that you don't have to adhere strictly to the ingredient lists and instructional steps provided. Some of the best dishes emerge when you take an existing recipe and modify it to your own tastes, so feel free to experiment!